'Probably the word "li
but left as an adjectiv
generosity. As a noun
incoherent bundle of positions, as chaotic as the opportunist
and value-free capitalism whose ally it so often is. This
incisive and intelligent book exposes with brilliant clarity the
failures of our current political culture, and outlines where
we should look for a political future that – for a change – has
something to do with the heart of human identity and human
desire. It obliges us to ask seriously what we have learned
about this in the collective trauma of the last year.'

Rowan Williams, former Archbishop of Canterbury

'Adrian Pabst is one of the most original and insightful thinkers
writing about politics today. In this book he examines the
challenges which technological change, environmental degra-
dation and unaccountable power pose to human flourishing.
You don't need to agree with his prescriptions to admire the
power of his diagnosis – this work is essential reading for all
concerned with our current discontents.'

**Rt Hon Michael Gove MP, Chancellor of the
Duchy of Lancaster**

'All thinking people realize that western liberal societies
face dilemmas they have been unable to resolve, but until
now there has been no constructive account of what a postliberal social order would look like. Adrian Pabst's brilliant
short book fills that gap. Fully recognizing the irreplaceable
achievements of liberalism, he argues compellingly that they
are endangered by an excessively individualist understanding
of human well being. By showing what this means in a wide
variety of fields, he has given us a book that advances understanding of the most fundamental issues of our time.'

**John Gray, philosopher and author of *Feline Philosophy:
Cats and the Meaning of Life***

'Adrian Pabst is one of our most interesting political thinkers – and this wise, compelling book provides not only a penetrating analysis of the crisis of liberalism but something much more valuable: a road map for a transformative politics. It should be essential reading for Keir Starmer – and indeed Boris Johnson.'

Jason Cowley, Editor of the *New Statesman*

'Within an impressive body of work this is Adrian Pabst's most political contribution to date. His ambition is to rethink the terms of what is known as postliberalism and anchor contemporary debate within certain distinct ethical traditions. He succeeds and in so doing performs the essential – and long overdue – task of reclaiming postliberalism from the right. This is a vital contribution to any renewed public philosophy for the left. After four defeats in just over a decade, here are the foundations of a coherent domestic and foreign policy reset for Labour.'

Jon Cruddas, Labour MP for Dagenham and Rainham and author of *The Dignity of Labour*

'A compelling case for a new politics based on the things that matter: families, places, traditions, relationships. This is the proper ground of political dispute – right and left should be fighting to represent the communitarian idea. Adrian Pabst has mapped the emerging post-liberal landscape with skill and passion. A vital book for the 2020s.'

Danny Kruger, Conservative MP for Devizes

'A common critique of 'post-liberal' writing is that it's stronger on critique than on vision. In the erudite but highly readable *Postliberal Politics*, Adrian Pabst seeks to remedy that shortcoming. Pabst draws on classical and Christian thinking to synthesise a vision for healthy public life after liberalism, that's neither narrowly nationalistic nor inhumanly globalised but ordered by solidarity both at local and international levels, and with our natural world. Readers on both Left and Right will find much in this timely book to challenge political preconceptions, and also to enrich and re-humanise an urgent political debate.'

Mary Harrington, UnHerd columnist

'By starting with the inescapability of limits and the common ground between liberal and authoritarian high-tech capitalism, Pabst succeeds with some flair in injecting political and intellectual substance into the idea of post-liberalism.'

Helen Thompson, Professor of Political Economy, University of Cambridge

'As the neoliberal consensus that provided the public philosophy of the post-Cold War West shatters, demagogic populism and authoritarianism threaten to take its place. Rejecting these dangerous alternatives, Adrian Pabst makes a persuasive case for rebuilding democracy on a foundation of strong communities.'

Michael Lind, author of *The New Class War: Saving Democracy from the Metropolitan Elite*

Postliberal Politics

Postliberal Politics

The Coming Era of Renewal

Adrian Pabst

polity

First published in 2021 by Polity Press

Polity Press
65 Bridge Street
Cambridge CB2 1UR, UK

Polity Press
101 Station Landing
Suite 300
Medford, MA 02155, USA

ISBN-13: 978-1-5095-4680-0
ISBN-13: 978-1-5095-4681-7 (pb)

A catalogue record for this book is available from the British Library.

Library of Congress Cataloging-in-Publication Data
Names: Pabst, Adrian, author.
Title: Postliberal politics : the coming communitarian consensus / Adrian
   Pabst.
Description: Cambridge, UK ; Medford, MA : Polity Press, 2021. | Includes
   bibliographical references and index. | Summary: "How to rebuild the
   common good beyond COVID-19, extreme identity politics, and free-market
   capitalism"-- Provided by publisher.
Identifiers: LCCN 2020057912 (print) | LCCN 2020057913 (ebook) | ISBN
   9781509546800 (hardback) | ISBN 9781509546817 (paperback) | ISBN
   9781509546824 (epub)
Subjects: LCSH: Consensus (Social sciences) | Communitarianism. | Common
   good. | Liberalism.
Classification: LCC JC328.2 .P32 2021 (print) | LCC JC328.2 (ebook) | DDC
   320.51/3--dc23
LC record available at https://lccn.loc.gov/2020057912
LC ebook record available at https://lccn.loc.gov/2020057913

Typeset in 11 on 13 pt Sabon
by Fakenham Prepress Solutions, Fakenham, Norfolk NR21 8NL
Printed and bound in the UK by TJ Books Ltd

For further information on Polity, visit our website:
politybooks.com

Contents

Contents

Preface

The idea for this book first emerged during a symposium on postliberal politics that took place in November 2019 at St George's House, Windsor Castle, at which it became clear that while postliberalism has a compelling critique of the discredited liberal consensus, which took the world by the scruff of the neck forty years ago, it lacks a convincing vision. A way through the political paralysis that has dominated the UK since the financial crisis and the shaping of a new era seemed a distant prospect. Barely a month later, the Conservative victory in the UK general election looked like a once-in-a-generation realignment of British politics, with working-class voters in Labour's former heartlands switching to the Tories and the Labour Party suffering its worst defeat since 1935.[1] A new winning consensus appeared to take shape: 'left on the economy' and 'right on culture'. But it was not postliberal.

From the outset, the Johnson government struggled to define a coherent position. It broke with the socio-economic liberalism of Blair and Cameron and combined Keynesian state activism with deregulated free trade. It flirted with social conservatism but embraced a brand of state centralism that undermines community and does little to support the family. Prior to the outbreak of Covid-19, I argued that the Tories had power without purpose: dreaming up revolutionary reforms that would unleash the forces of technology and accelerated capitalism and so deepen divisions just when the country needs a national politics of the common good.[2] It was disruption for its own sake with ill-thought-out Hayekian antecedents.

The pandemic further exposed Conservative confusion: caught between libertarian instincts and statist solutions; appearing to 'follow the science' but breaking lockdown rules; hostile to local devolution yet incompetent centralizers; invoking the 'will of the people' while failing to foster communal solidarity. What does 'levelling up' actually imply? But the Tories are not alone in lacking a noticeable *telos*. Across the West, liberals are doubling down on the failed fusion of technocracy with ultra-progressivism. National populists champion the power of strongmen who deploy state coercion and erode constitutional norms. Behind their version of 'left on the economy' and 'right on culture' lurk forms of statism and moralism that will do nothing to secure shared prosperity or plural societies.

Despite their differences, each of contemporary liberalism, populism and authoritarianism threaten democracy and pluralism.[3] They converge around state centralization, crony capitalism, tech surveillance and rival versions of the 'culture wars' that fuel each other – a major theme of the book. This convergence opens up a space for a politics of place and people entrusted with power and resources to shape their everyday lives; an industrial strategy to build national resilience; and a new social covenant to try to repair broken communities and recreate a shared sense of belonging and duty.

Preface

Such a politics is anti-authoritarian but not anti-liberal. On the contrary, liberty and fundamental rights are precious gifts that should not be curtailed. Yet they can only be sustained by the practice of fraternity and mutual obligations. Genuine postliberalism draws on the best liberal traditions but corrects liberal errors and excesses such as individualism, untrammelled capitalism or identity politics. Its organizing principles are community, mutual markets, ethical enterprise and the common purposes around which people associate. In short, a postliberal politics that seeks to build new robust communities.

No political party or government has so far embraced genuine postliberalism by combining economic justice with social solidarity and ecological balance – the other major theme of the book. Building on postliberal thought and its philosophical forebears, my aim is to develop a political and policy programme anchored in a public philosophy of the good life. A good life, like the common good, involves a plural search for shared ends that bind us together as social beings: the quest for individual fulfilment together with mutual flourishing; a degree of personal autonomy within engaged and convivial societies; and common prosperity as part of a blossoming biosphere. The good life requires a civic covenant – a partnership between generations, between regions, between nations and with nature. This is only unrealistic as long as we accept the dominant assumptions. Covid-19 has exposed the weaknesses of the current ideologies and revealed the deep desire for security and solidarity. Now is the time. Let us build that new covenant.

Adrian Pabst
Muswell Hill
March 2021

Acknowledgements

I owe a debt of gratitude to many people who have helped me to complete this book. Particular thanks go to my colleagues at the University of Kent and at the National Institute of Economic and Social Research for their support, especially Iain MacKenzie, Jane O'Mahony and Richard Whitman at Kent as well as Jagjit Chadha and Hande Küçük at NIESR. I am also very grateful to the participants of the 2019 symposium on postliberal politics at Windsor, notably Phillip Blond, Peter Franklin, Giles Fraser, John Gray, Mary Harrington, Julius Krein, Michael Merrick, Aris Roussinos, Freddie Sayers, Will Tanner, Helen Thompson, Ed West and the late Wendy Wheeler, who is much missed.

Many ideas in these pages took shape in conversations with my comrades Richard Beardsworth, Susannah Black, Jon Cruddas, Fred Dallmayr, Ruth Davis, Paul Embery, Tobias Fibbs, Maurice Glasman, Jack Hutchinson, Wayne Hudson, Shabana Mahmood, John Milbank, Jonathan Rutherford and Liam Stokes. I owe an exceptional debt of gratitude to six friends who read (parts of) the manuscript: Christopher Coker, Jason Cowley, Ron Ivey, James Noyes, Sebastian Milbank and

Acknowledgements

Richard Sawka. Their generous comments improved both style and substance, and Sebastian taught me the difference between good and bad alliteration! Of course, not all of the arguments developed here reflect their views.

I could not have written the book without the ceaseless encouragement and counsel of my publisher George Owers. It has been a pleasure working with him and his dedicated colleagues Julia Davies and Rachel Moore at Polity. Thanks must also go to Justin Dyer, whose copy-editing was brilliant.

My greatest debt is to my wife Elena and our children Alexander and Katya for their unfailing patience and love. It is to them that I dedicate the book. *Deo gratias.*

Prologue: a new era

For a brief moment in 2020, it seemed as if the long interregnum that began with the 2008 financial crash might finally end. After years of austerity and anger, the Covid-19 pandemic brought people together by acts of quiet generosity. Our polarized politics gave way to national unity as we rediscovered a sense of shared purpose: acting in solidarity to slow the infection rate and save lives. In neighbourhoods and across nations, people volunteered to deliver food and medicines to the vulnerable and those experiencing poverty or loneliness. Governments of all stripes paid the wages of workers and provided emergency loans for businesses. The coronavirus crisis brought out the great human spirit of decency, fraternity and kindness. Our response during the first lockdown was a communitarian moment.

Yet it proved to be a false dawn. The winners of the shutdown were tech oligarchs such as Amazon, Google or China's Alibaba while family-owned businesses folded and inner-city shops were boarded up. And following the brutal police killing of George Floyd in the US, a wave of protests and counter-protests once more poisoned the public realm, backed by big business and fuelled by a culture of abuse on social media. After a short period of compassion and community, hyper-capitalism and extreme identity politics were back with a vengeance. Both are destroying the basis of a common life shared across ages and classes.[1] What comes next will be different from what came before, but the 'new normal' is largely an intensification of the forces that dominated the old status quo: capitalism, nationalism and technocracy. Instead of resolving the interregnum, politics seems caught in an impasse.

Across the West, the old opposition of left versus right has been supplanted by a new polarity of liberal versus populist, but neither appears to be capable of defining a new position except negatively and by demonizing the other. The stand-off between the old establishment and the new insurgent elites leaves little space for decent leadership or real democracy.[2] In China and the 'rising rest', authoritarian one-party rule is fusing state capitalism with nationalism in ways that deny funda-mental freedoms and supress democratic movements. In response to the paralysed liberal order and a divided West, the challengers in Eurasia portray themselves as peaceful civilizational states that supposedly combine pre-liberal civilization with modern statehood.[3] In reality, authoritarians sow discord at home and abroad while dressing up their demagogy as strength compared with liberal-democratic weakness.

Locked in a national and global struggle, none of the three dominant ideologies looks set to be hegemonic: liberalism neither dies nor renews itself; populism is effective at ejecting liberals from office but in power amounts to little more than complacent boosterism; authoritarianism taunts Western democracy without offering any viable long-term alternative to the challenges of the modern world.

Prologue

The Covid-19 pandemic is a crossroads: a moment of decision about journeys taken and prospects ignored. We can either revert to liberal individualism, or slide ever more into demagogic populism, or accelerate towards authoritarian control. Alternatively, we could build a politics on the things that matter to people: our families and friends; the places where we live and work; the relationships of support and community that sustain us; and the institutions that provide security. Key to this conception of politics is the idea that we are embodied beings who flourish when we are embedded in interpersonal relationships and institutions giving us meaning as well as agency. Such a politics is postliberal and communitarian – one that avoids the excesses of liberalism without succumbing to the errors of populism or the oligarchic criminality of authoritarianism.

Communitarian postliberalism

Postliberal thought is not new, and it draws on intellectual traditions stretching back to Aristotle, Catholic social thought and communitarianism.[4] But in recent years it has too often become associated with a politics that is antiliberal and antimodern, animated by a reactionary desire to roll back the new rights of minorities and to return to social and political exclusion along the axes of race, sex or class. A true postliberal approach eschews crude forms of solidarity built on ethnic or religious homogeneity and instead embraces the pluralist heritage of ethical traditions forged in the nineteenth and the twentieth century – including personalism, one-nation conservatism and ethical socialism.

Prologue

The postliberal politics which this book develops is emphatically not antiliberal. Rather, it begins with a sense of the limits of the liberal project: the damage done by individualism; liberty reduced to the removal of constraints on private choice; individual rights disconnected from mutual obligations; the erosion of intermediary institutions by the combined power of the free market aided by the centralized state; global disorder based on coercion, trade deficits and permanent war.[5] By contrast, postliberalism views human beings as relational and freedom as a balance between autonomy and self-restraint. Rights are not just indissociable from duties but also ineffective without them. States and markets only generate shared prosperity together with social cohesion when they are embedded in strong civic institutions and structures of self-help that sustain a sense of belonging. A genuine international order requires cooperation between nations and peoples anchored in social and cultural ties, fair trade as well as military restraint.[6]

Postliberal politics is communitarian in new ways. It links the deep desire for community that was manifest during the first lockdown to the recognition that most people belong to more than one community and that they are also part of free, newly shaped associations beyond given communities. The communitarianism which this book defends is also corporatist and internationalist. Democratic corporatism seeks to reconcile the estranged interests of government, business and organized labour. To protect people from the pressures of state and market power, we need to strengthen all the intermediary institutions that help constitute society: trade unions, universities, local authorities, business associations, faith communities, as well as all other components of our social fabric like pubs, post

4

offices and public libraries. And since this cannot be done within the boundaries of nation-states or by one country alone, we also need a new account of international relations and global politics.[7]

A new era

To resist the temptations of reverting to technocratic liberalism or sliding into authoritarianism, communitarian postliberalism requires a shared political and policy programme anchored in a public philosophy. At the heart of it is a vision of national renewal based on a reconstruction of our shared interests and underpinned by principles of contributive justice and reciprocal obligations. Instead of pinning our hopes on a single political leader or party, we need to build a broad communitarian consensus that puts society above politics and the economy, rebuilding the social fabric that binds communities and countries together. Postliberalism recognizes the true purpose of politics as the conciliation of estranged interests through the pursuit of the common good. The economy only works well when it serves shared prosperity rather than vested interests. All this has to be translated into public policy, joined up to combine greater economic justice with more social stability and ecological balance.

The national interest is intertwined with international solidarity. Nations and peoples, sometimes under religious inspiration, form bonds of trust and cooperation with one another within states but equally across borders. The nation-state and the working classes have not been and should not be swept away by globalization or the rise of a professional-managerial class, but going forward the task is to forge new cross-class and cross-cultural coalitions both nationally and internationally. Postliberal politics promotes an internationalist vision anchored in nations and civic institutions as a constructive alternative to globalism and nationalism; of an international order founded on establishing trust and friendship rather than calculated self-interest.

A novel popular consensus is necessary to resolve the interregnum: the period between the previous and the next settlement. Liberalism's old hegemony has ended but not yet been replaced by a new worldview. To command majority support, politics has to start with what most people value: family, friendship, locality, community and country. Reasonable hope for a better future has to be rooted in ways of life that involve a sense of sacrifice and contribution to the common good. It is about cherishing freedom, a sense of fair play and the places and concrete communities where people live. All these values rest on lived solidarity: relationships of 'give-and-receive' that give our daily lives meaning.

For all the suffering it has brought, the Covid-19 pandemic represents a moment to rebuild the common life which lies at the heart of a healthy body politic. Now is the time for such an alternative that is centred on trust, dignity and human relationships. The coronavirus crisis could further accelerate the dominant forces of our age, or it could herald something more hopeful: a new era of renewal.

I

POSTLIBERAL TIMES

Have we not been here before? Ever since the 2008 financial crisis, economic liberalism has been in question. The 2011 Tottenham riots, which spread to other parts of Britain, shone a light on community breakdown and the limits of social liberalism.[1] Five years later, after the Brexit vote and Donald Trump's victory, the populist backlash was not merely a rejection of the consensus based on the double liberalism championed by *The Economist*. More importantly, it was also a stirring of the double desire for earning and belonging – the dignity of work and a sense of shared identity.[2] Both are grounded in a quest for esteem and recognition.

Yet in each instance, party politics did not live up to the task. Red Tory and Blue Labour had some intellectual influence on David Cameron's Big Society narrative and Ed Miliband's vision of One Nation Labour, but the party leaders and their main advisers retreated to variants of progressivism as the default setting. In the wake of the Brexit vote, Theresa May tried but failed to develop a new working-class conservative politics that rejected Thatcherite economics and Cameron's modernization drive in favour of a more traditional Toryism that accentuates the good that government can do to make markets work while also repairing the social fabric. As the *Guardian* columnist Martin Kettle suggested back in 2016,

> These are still early days, but May's speeches, both before and after becoming prime minister, are unified by postliberal thinking. [...] Brexit is in part a revolt against a set of characteristics of modern liberalism. We have a new political agenda that no political party can afford to ignore. Whether we consider ourselves liberal or not, we increasingly inhabit postliberal times.[3]

Not unlike Miliband and Cameron before her, however, May abandoned a postliberal vision of renewal in favour of a position defined by the old orthodoxies of the free market supported by the bureaucratic state. Her government watered down industrial policy and corporate governance reform while pursuing free-trade deals for a Global Britain that were disconnected from the national economy.[4] A lack of intellectual depth combined with poor leadership sealed her fate.

Since then, people's support for populists such as Donald Trump, Matteo Salvini, Giorgia Meloni (the leader of the far-right Brothers of Italy party), Jair Bolsonaro or Boris Johnson has not been matched by a coherent politics or policy programme to tackle legitimate grievances to which progressive politics – from Bill Clinton via Tony Blair to Barack Obama and David Cameron – contributed significantly during the two decades of rampant globalization. Yet for all their rhetoric about defending 'the will of the people' against corrupt elites, populists have done little to address the resentment and humiliation experienced by millions. The long interregnum that began in the wake of the financial crisis has not been decisively resolved by the populist insurgency. Meanwhile liberals are not taking their defeat lying down. The liberal counter-putsch we saw with the protests following the violent death of George Floyd is ultimately part of the same culture war on which demagogic populists thrive.[5] The postliberal times we entered a decade ago are still with us, and Covid-19 is another moment in their unfolding.

1

Resolving the interregnum

During weeks of lies and cover-up about Covid-19 by the Chinese government, international flights out of the epicentre in China's Hubei province continued to operate, turning a local plague into a global pandemic. When Wuhan was finally closed off, videos emerged of the local authorities forcibly removing residents from their homes and rounding up suspected carriers of the virus. As people were sent to mass quarantine camps, they were told that lockdown was for the good of the community and the state, equated with the Communist Party. Beijing's primary concern was economic growth and the image of the ruling regime. In the West, the US and UK governments delayed the lockdown as they initially seemed to privilege population-wide 'herd immunity' to protect the economy. This amounted to a policy that could have seen hundreds of thousands of weaker members of society die.

While the early response of the Chinese showed merciless indifference to the human suffering of Wuhan's population, that of the US and the UK was built on economism and utility. Either way, a sacrificial logic was at work that put material and ideological interests ahead of human survival and security. The coronavirus crisis has exposed the limitations of both China's model and that of the Anglo-Saxon West. Neither model addresses the underlying conditions that left us vulnerable to pandemics like Covid-19: an overcentralized state eroding local institutions; globalized markets diminishing the resilience of the national economy; hollowed-out civic institutions combined with weak relationships of trust and obligation.

The past forty years have been dominated first by ultraliberalism in the West and then by antiliberal authoritarianism in China. Events of the past decade – from the 2008 global financial crash to Brexit and Trump, from the rise of Xi Jinping to the pandemic – have revealed the weaknesses of both systems. They are vulnerable to the forces of capitalism, nationalism and techno-science. No alternative ideology has so far captured the popular imagination or built a consensus capable of commanding majority support. We seem stuck in an interregnum where the old order has collapsed but not been replaced by a new settlement. In the words of the Italian philosopher Antonio Gramsci, who coined this term, 'The crisis consists precisely in the fact that the old is dying and the new cannot be born; in this interregnum morbid phenomena of the most varied kind come to pass.'[1]

Zombie order

We still live in the long interregnum that began with the financial crisis. No single ideology or system has supplanted the dominance of liberalism since the Soviet Communist implosion in 1989. In the West, national populism is here to stay but struggles to govern and address the grievances of its new working-class base.

China and other authoritarian regimes flex their economic muscle but lack the independent institutions and social trust on which vibrant societies depend. While the American-led Atlantic era is fading, the Chinese or Asian century has not yet begun. The paroxysm of pandemic and protest that we witnessed in the US and the UK may end up being the defining moment in the decline of the liberal West, but is it a prelude to the death of liberalism itself? That is the fear of the Western establishment, who see the return of 1930s totalitarian rule in every populist insurgency. It is the hope of the West's rivals in Moscow, Beijing and beyond, for whom America's mutation into a semi-failed state confirms the superiority of authoritarianism.

But besides the demise of the West and the rise of the rest, there is another possibility. The Western liberal order will continue to stagger on – sclerotic yet stoic, decadent yet durable, inert without either real reform or complete collapse. 'That may well be the fate of the liberal order over the next generations,' writes the American commentator Ross Douthat, 'a kind of sustainable decadence, a zombie existence punctuated by periods of temporary crisis and alarm that continues indefinitely.'[2] As the post-viral economic cataclysm unfolds, the liberal West looks like the undead: not coming back to life but equally refusing to die.

Could the populist insurgency revitalize the West? Up to a point it has proven to be a corrective to some excesses of liberalism such as austerity, job-exporting trade deals and pressure on wages as a result of mass immigration. Yet going left on the economy and right on identity is hardly the same as a new political consensus. That would require a coherent governing philosophy, but unlike the neoliberal model of Thatcher and Reagan, which drew on thirty years of Hayekian

13

thinking, populists lack the intellectual resources to build a different settlement. With few exceptions, left populism has not survived contact with actual voters. Right populism, by contrast, is successful in ejecting liberal elites from power and has an inkling of what needs to be done. Yet it lacks the concepts and policy tools to bring about transformative change.

This is perhaps most apparent in its failure to take on crony capitalism. Populists of different stripes in Poland, Hungary and Brazil fund increased state spending with foreign capital based on low tax and deregulatory incentives. Competitive fiscal dumping is part of protectionism, besides a clampdown on cheap foreign labour. The national-populist alternative to liberal hyper-globalization is market nativism disguised as the promise of economic patriotism. In times of polarization, populists resort to Leninist tactics of political purges and institution-wrecking while people yearn for a measure of economic and social stability.

As the academic Michael Lind has argued, insurgents are right to oppose technocratic neoliberalism but wrong to embrace what he calls demagogic populism.[3] Populists are just as elite as the establishment. Both have failed to offer a political vision that is anchored in a sense of the transcendent 'we' – the bonds of belonging to neighbourhoods and nations. Instead, the ultraliberal left and the antiliberal right indulge in variants of identity politics that fuel each other. Both erode the cultural and civilizational foundations of the West, a sense of common purpose and shared destiny.[4]

Whether the Western imperium disintegrates or reinvents itself, the authoritarian alternative is unlikely to displace liberal democracy altogether. Both China and Russia are already struggling with the effects of deglobalization: from new trade barriers to the loss of foreign direct investment and of technological transfer.[5] The worst global economic downturn since the Great Depression of 1929–32 will likely reverse rising living standards for some time and diminish the greater international prestige on which one-party state rule rests. With hour-glass social structures and a new class of rapacious oligarchs, China will double down on its fusion of state capitalism with bio-surveillance. Anglo-Saxon capitalism could yet prove more resilient and innovative than Leninist tech totalitarianism.

Liberalism, populism and authoritarianism will endure, just as patterns of daily life will be re-established and old habits will take hold of us once again. Pandemics or protests pose no existential threat to liberal empire, populist power or authoritarian regimes. No governments or political systems have so far fallen. The strange non-death of economic globalization, which brought about the financial crash of 2008, testifies to the durability of capitalism, which is compatible with variously more market-driven or state-orchestrated systems. Far from collapsing under the weight of its own inner contradictions, global capitalism continues to expand and is sustained by a novel mix of Hayekian ultra-loose monetary policy with Keynesian state subsidy. Capitalism is not just built on greed, debt and destruction. It is also politically promiscuous, getting into bed with any ideology – liberal, populist or authoritarian – that backs the impersonal forces of finance capital and techno-science at the expense of the dignity of labour and democratic self-government.

Since the end of the Soviet bloc and the crushing of the Chinese democracy movement in 1989, both liberals and authoritarians have tolerated grotesque disparities of power, wealth and social status while proffering the myth of meritocracy. Now the fallout from the pandemic threatens a decade of discontent. For all these reasons, Covid-19 may change little except to intensify existing and sinister political-economic developments, tending to both mass surveillance and mutual atomization.[6] The West is stuck in limbo between a populist insurgency and a counter-putsch by the neoliberal establishment. Meanwhile authoritarian systems combine political stagnation at home with aggressive expansion abroad. How to resolve the interregnum?

A postliberal space

Yet the current crisis can also be seen as an exception that suspends previous norms and received wisdom: ever-greater globalization; endless mobility; the hollowing out of the state and the public realm; treating nature as a consumable resource; or elevating the individual will into the highest moral arbiter. For those lucky enough to be able to work from home, a relaxation from the rigour of exhausting commutes, time-starved lifestyles and over-priced Pret lunches wolfed down while checking email has given rise to a rethinking of priorities. Are high salaries worth it if they come at the cost of being a stranger to one's own children, raised chiefly in nurseries? What will it profit a woman or man if she or he gains the next promotion, but loses her or his family life? To those who had no choice but to continue to go to work – the heroic but underpaid shop-workers, nurses, bus drivers and so forth – the crisis heightened the importance of their vocation and contribution, exposing the fallacy that the labour market rewards the most useful or meritorious members of the community most highly.[7]

The pandemic and the first lockdown created the conditions in which to rethink all these things and more.

The journalist Jason Cowley expresses this hopefulness well: '[C]ommunity was being rediscovered through enforced social isolation – consider those 750,000 volunteers for the NHS. The pandemic had created the conditions in which to rethink everything – our relationship to one another and to nature; our economic and political settlement; our national and international priorities.'[8] As we confront existential questions about our frailty and mortality, our politics of left/right or liberal/authoritarian are fast becoming obsolete. None of the ideological options on offer provide a sense of personal, national or international renewal.

A space is opening up for an alternative that avoids both these extremes and offers an ethical compass with which to navigate our times: postliberalism.[9] Postliberalism is not a homogeneous movement but begins with a shared sense of the failure of the liberal project and the pressing need to sustain its best aspects in a new form. Liberalism with its various strands is not all bad, and some of the institutions it has built will rightly endure, including better access to the rule of law, the free press, greater freedoms and individual rights, as well as protection of minorities. But not only is liberal ideology contradictory, because the inevitable clash of rival rights can only be arbitrated by collective power. It is also the case that liberty, once disconnected from self-restraint and mutual obligation, slides into unfreedom – even tyranny – because unfettered freedom favours the strong over the weak, the wealthy over the poor, the powerful over those without a voice. The self-erosion of liberal values such as freedom, equality, tolerance and pluralism reflects pathologies that at once distort liberalism's principles yet reveal the logic of liberal ideology. The American political philosopher Patrick Deneen puts this well:

> Liberalism has failed – not because it fell short, but because it was true to itself. It failed because it has succeeded. […] A political philosophy that was launched to foster greater equity, defend a pluralist tapestry of different cultures and beliefs, protect human dignity, and, of course, expand liberty, in practice generates titanic inequality, enforces uniformity and homogeneity, fosters material and spiritual degradation, and undermines freedom.[10]

And for all the advances they have brought, liberal societies, as the philosopher John Gray remarked at the 2019 Windsor symposium on postliberal renewal, form an inheritance that needs to be repaired and amended if it is to renew itself and survive into the future. On current evidence, the reimagining of liberalism is not about to happen, as most attempts either buy into the liberal premise that the economy trumps culture, which ignores the importance of mutual recognition, or else accept the primacy of the individual and negative liberty, which ends in the individualism that has destroyed any prospects of shared prosperity and social cohesion.[11] Liberalism's worst excesses will continue to destroy the cultural and religious roots on which it depends: the trust, cooperation and participation of people in decision-making that are vital for the functioning of liberal institutions.

The most thoughtful interventions on renewing liberalism, such as the essay by the academic Timothy Garton Ash in early 2021, recognize the limits of liberal liberty, yet their appeal to the practice of self-restraint draws on the conservative yearning for community and the socialist disposition towards lived solidarity.[12] This suggests not only that a 'liberalism of hope' is always already hybrid hut also that the future of politics is paradoxical – not the false binary of liberal thinking

18

that opposes the individual to the collective, the market to the state or liberal democracy to antiliberal authoritarianism. Whereas these opposites end up coinciding (as argued in chapter 3) and liberalism slides into libertarian or authoritarian ideology, the new politics centres on the person, the civic institutions that help give people agency and a popular democracy combined with virtuous leadership. Postliberalism is no perfect name, but far from revealing its 'epigonic character', as Garton Ash alleges, it describes a new space after the hegemony of liberalism and moves the debate onto the novel battleground between one-nation conservatism and ethical socialism.

What postliberalism is and isn't

Postliberalism rests on a recognition that society is not founded upon an impersonal social contract between individuals, as for liberal thought since Hobbes and Locke, but emerges from a reciprocal covenant between the generations. Liberty is not freedom from obligations or freedom for selfish interests but a freedom of care for oneself and for others. Individual fulfilment based on personal autonomy has to be balanced with mutual flourishing. Equality is not sameness but a respect for the basic and integral dignity of everyone: their body, mind and soul. Individual rights should not be rolled back but rather made concrete and relational by linking them to obligations towards others.

Postliberals believe in fundamental fair play: that rules are binding on all and that privileges have to be earned. Connected with this is a sense of contributive justice: that duties beget rights and that we are most fully human when we earn the esteem of our fellow citizens for the contributions we make to society's common good through our work and our care for others. As the moral philosopher Michael Sandel writes: '[T]he fundamental human need is to be needed by those with whom we share a common life.'[13] In an age of deep division and humiliation, postliberals agree that the task is to rebuild a common life by repairing relationships and renewing institutions that command our attachment and affection: pubs, post offices and parks, sports clubs, public libraries and the high street, hospitals, schools and the workplace, but equally local government, the armed forces, symbols of patriotism and international cooperation.

The disagreements among postliberals reflect different philosophical and political commitments. Some postliberals are religious, others are not, but all respect religion as a source of meaning and a pillar of a stable society. Some postliberals come from the right or the left of the political spectrum, while others identify with the radical centre. Some postliberals reject liberalism as intellectually and morally bankrupt, while others seek to reform the liberal tradition from within. All agree that liberal ideals of freedom, equality, the rule of law, representative government and individual rights can only be defended with the help of social virtues such as fraternity, duty, loyalty, humility and honour.

The danger confronting postliberals is that some of them will succumb to the pressures of liberal centrism while others will be seduced by the lure of demagogic populism or outright authoritarianism. To hold the line, postliberals need to resist simplistic slogans, chief of all 'going left on the economy and right on culture'. Neither social conservatism nor economic statism provides answers to our problems: society is already too atomized to be simply conserved while statist solutions will leave us yet more powerless – stripped of agency and deprived of dignity. Instead of social conservatism, postliberalism seeks to rebuild community and nurture our ability to live fulfilled lives in common. And instead of economic statism, postliberalism promotes a corporatist model that is democratic and internationalist, reconstructing the everyday economy and the national economy combined with international institutions to constrain capital.

Some self-styled postliberals claim that the left is too wedded to socio-cultural liberalism to embrace a postliberal politics of communal solidarity, whereas the right has already moved beyond deregulated capitalism. They point to the examples of Poland and Hungary, which combine a protectionist state with pro-family welfare and education policies. But this glosses over the fact that the Polish and Hungarian models are a form of state capitalism largely reliant on fiscal dumping and deregulation to attract foreign capital while sliding into authoritarian nationalism that undermines constitutional freedoms.

And the claim that it is easier for the right to move left on economics and public services than it is for the left to move right on culture and identity ignores the reality of contemporary right-wing governments. They are mostly variants of state-market power that are economically liberal (as with Keynesian spending) and socially antiliberal (as with Trump and aspects of the Hungarian and Polish governments) – not genuinely postliberal. Behind the simplistic slogan 'left on the economy and right on culture' lurks an admiration for a politics of state control and the rule of strongmen. The ruling parties of Poland and Hungary, which have fostered a climate of impunity for virulent nationalism and anti-Semitism, are not exactly paragons of Christian democracy. A truly postliberal party or government is yet to emerge.

In conclusion: the coronavirus crisis shines a light on the underlying conditions or co-morbidities of our bodies and our body politic. It risks amplifying and accelerating the forces of capitalism, bio-surveillance and identity politics that leave our societies more fragmented and fragile. Yet the political space for a paradoxical politics both radical and traditional still exists.[14] Only a politics that fuses economic justice with social solidarity and ecological balance can build a cross-class coalition defending the interests of a popular majority. That would resolve the interregnum and give meaning to the postliberal times we live in.

2

Politics after the plague

In his novel *The Plague* (*La peste*), Albert Camus captures the meaning of the Covid-19 pandemic in our times: 'There were no longer any individual destinies, but a collective history that was the plague, and feelings shared by all. The greatest of these were feelings of separation and exile, with all that that involved of fear and rebellion.'[1] The coronavirus pestilence demands a particular sacrifice: solidarity through separation. We are not just reminded of our vulnerability and mutual dependence, but also required to abandon our workplace, suspend our social life and stay at home in order to save lives. Paradoxically, 'we are all in this together' by staying apart. The new-found community rests on 'social distancing' for fear of contagion.

Covid-19 has affected all of us, everywhere and at the same time, attacking our pre-existing weaknesses and disrupting ways of life. That is not the same as the bubonic plagues in the Middle Ages that decimated Europe's population or the European viruses during the Age of Discovery that ravaged Latin America. Both those killed people in their millions and left civiliz-ations fundamentally transformed. The Black Death ended serfdom and revalued human labour, whereas

Iberian-imported diseases wiped out indigenous people and ushered in centuries of Western colonialism. The coronavirus does not mark the end of the West and the rise of 'the rest', though it might accelerate Western self-erosion and China's ascendancy. The communitarian consensus that was manifest during the first lockdown could also renew the West's best traditions.

Human decency

What the present plague certainly does is to reveal the fragility of our human and social condition. It works on the body politic in the same way as on our physical bodies, probing our immune system and preying upon underlying co-morbidities, as the political theorist and Labour peer Maurice Glasman has argued.[2] The pandemic has laid bare the erosion of our everyday economy, stripped down to 'just-in-time' delivery and dependent on foreign powers we cannot trust. Covid-19 has also shone a light on the hollowing out of society, built on an atrophied polity and anaemic civic institutions. For decades, state and market concentrated wealth, power and status. Now the coronavirus crisis amplifies the unravelling of our structures. Entire countries need debt-based life support and people are forced into protective isolation. Vulnerability has been shown to be the fundamental reality of our lives. Yet frailty is also what makes us human.

Unlike his erstwhile friend Jean-Paul Sartre, Camus was no follower of atheist Marxism. One of the thinkers who influenced him most on the question of human weakness was St Augustine. Camus' literary œuvre is a long reflection on this and other existential questions: our mortality, our humanity, the hopes and fears of our earthly existence. Without being a confessing Christian, he was sympathetic to a broad Christian humanist vision, which he viewed as standing apart from both reactionary clericalism and scientific atheism. Camus rejected Marxist and liberal ideologies alike, opposing at once the apologists of the Soviet Union for equating oppression with liberation and liberals for abandoning a common ethical outlook in favour of individual greed and selfishness.

Contemporary liberals seem unable to defend freedom as a form of ethical restraint that respects the limits of life. Liberty is instead reduced either to a utilitarian pursuit of pleasure and prosperity or else to absolute legal injunction. For this reason, advocates of ultra-liberalism are the first ones to fall victim to a plague: 'They considered themselves free,' Camus writes, 'and no one will ever be free as long as there is plague, pestilence and famine.'[3] Human existence is about frailty as much as freedom. During the Covid-19 pandemic, the deep desire for community has been palpable. Whereas liberals oscillate between free choice and total lockdown, communities want greater state protection combined with more social solidarity.

The ultraliberal longing for limitless liberty is what Camus would call absurd because it is meaningless. Untrammelled freedom dehumanizes us, replacing our contingent condition with a determinism that robs us of our own agency. Nor are we humans immortal or invincible – forms of hubris that come with conceit, the pursuit of possessions and striving for status, a lack of joy and an absence of gratitude. Camus' sceptical humanism is a call against ancient pagan heroism as much as modern self-assertion. Missing from these two conceptions of ethics are basic moral sentiments that define our humanity. This is reflected in the words of

Dr Rieux, the central character in Camus' novel, who believes the plague brings into sharp relief the nature of our human condition: '[T]his whole thing is not about heroism, it is about decency [*honnêteté*]. It may seem a ridiculous idea, but the only way to fight the plague is with decency.'[4]

The dignity of life and labour

When asked what decency is, he replies: 'In general, I can't say, but in my case I know that it consists in doing my job [*métier*].'[5] Camus links this to uncertainty: 'Rieux shook himself. This was certainty: everyday work. The rest hang by threads and imperceptible movements; one could not dwell on it. The main thing was to do one's job well.'[6] Trying to do one's job well is to be a hero of the everyday. During the Covid-19 pandemic, doctors on the intensive care units of countless hospitals across the world worked heroically to save the lives of thousands. Yet, as shown by Edward Docx's extraordinary essay in the *New Statesman* on the experience of an intensive care consultant, '[T]he truth is that the people who watch the patients are the nurses. Hour after hour into the night – an unceasing vigil.'[7] For a brief period, the weekly clapping for carers in the UK united people in moments of spontaneous solidarity around a shared gratitude for the sacrifice and service of key workers.

After decades of being told that the new knowledge economy is driven by the professional-managerial class largely composed of bankers and lawyers, we now realize who the essential workers are. Lorry drivers and warehouse workers. Delivery staff and shelf-stackers. Shop assistants and cashiers. Police officers and firefighters. Doctors and nurses. Hospital cleaners and home carers. 'Labour,' writes Glasman, 'is something you can't do from home. It requires real physical presence, leaving home and doing something, usually involving your hands, for other people. Far from being replaced by machines, key workers require skill, empathy and compassion to fulfil their vocation.'[8] The Covid-19 pandemic has created the conditions for restoring the meaning and dignity of labour. The labour value has been revealed as central to the economy and society. It is through work that we find fulfilment and become more human.[9]

Frailty, decency, sacrifice, service and the dignity of labour are some of the building blocks for a post-pandemic politics that is guided by an ethical compass. It is a re-moralized politics that transcends the pursuit of power or wealth by helping people to live rewarding lives for themselves and others. The vocation of politics is not to endorse a single conception of the good life or to impose moralistic values. Rather, it is to enable people to live both in security, free from fear or want, and in dignity. Like the idea of the good life, dignity is not reducible to one thing. Sometimes, it is painfully expressed in grief when we experience dispossession or the loss of loved ones. At other times, it is celebrated joyously when we can exercise agency and shape the world around us. In each case, dignity concerns both one's own intrinsic worth and the worth of others. It is about earning esteem and recognizing contribution.[10]

Security and dignity frame questions of justice, which exceed individual rights or collective utility. Justice is about relations within society and how they should be organized so that people can live fulfilling lives. Covid-19 has brought this to the fore. The initial response to the pandemic was to privilege health and well-being over economic growth. As we recognize the need to move from 'just-in-time' supply chains to 'just-in-case' safety nets, so too we must replace 'business as usual' with ethical firms and new ways of value creation. For now, austerity has been consigned to the dustbin of history (though libertarians and Thatcherites are itching to bring it back). The size and role of the state in the economy will continue to grow over the next few years. A space is opening up for novel economic and political arrangements anchored in the public good. That means reconciling estranged interests between capital, labour and the state. It also involves infusing greater social and ecological purpose into both business and the public sector.

Change of era

As Pope Francis remarked, we are witnessing not an era of change but a change of era. The virus speeds up long-standing developments that have been decades in the making: the fragmentation of free-market globalization and the resurgence of the protective state; a greater emphasis on borders and national sovereignty; the need for greater investment in our public services and the importance of civic community; the urgency for science and technology to serve human needs in a manner that favours ecological balance; a yearning for stability and mass participation in big ways and small to take care of others.

Each of these developments is consistent with principles of liberality like pluralism, tolerance and generosity, and yet none of them are reflected in contemporary liberalism. All of these developments involve some respect for authority within bounded

28

polities – respect for law and order as well as for the inheritance of customs and traditions. Yet none of them are honoured by authoritarianism with its antiliberal attack on certain rights and institutions, including the free press or the independent judiciary. Potentially, these developments represent a new reality that is postliberal – fusing greater economic justice with social stability and ecological purpose. But each development and the wider world that might take shape after the viral emergency can go one of three ways: either reverting to the well-trodden path of liberalism, or sliding towards the cliff-edge of antiliberalism, or taking the road of postliberalism.

The first development is the fragmenting of the global economy. Before the outbreak of the Covid-19 crisis, the pace of economic globalization was slowing down. Since 2015, the rate has flattened as cross-border financial flows first stagnated and then fell. The US–China trade spat has the potential to disrupt global commerce. Outsourcing labour and offshoring production will continue to cost corporations as the post-pandemic emphasis shifts towards national resilience and more local supply chains. Ruchir Sharma, a writer and economist at Morgan Stanley, argues that these developments are a corrective of free-market globalism. Far from being temporary setbacks, they have the potential to transform the world economy in the direction of what he calls deglobalization.[11] But at a time when the post-1989 era of neoliberal triumph has ended, global capitalism is not about to collapse.

Paradoxically, antiliberal protectionism may save the current economic order from some of its own worst excesses that have stymied national development. Deglobalizing tendencies are not by themselves a harbinger of postliberal times. That would involve a balancing of greater national economic autonomy with more international cooperation to secure the status of workers and enable them to resist the dehumanizing exploitation of contemporary capitalism by building new forms of democratic association – starting with trade unions in the big tech and gig economies (especially Amazon) and allowing worker self-organization in state capitalist countries like China.

The second development is the resurgence of the protective state, which is similar to what happened seventy-five years ago. Then the shared experience of mass participation in the Second World War was key to the birth of the post-war social settlement based on state intervention in the economy and welfare support from 'cradle to grave'. Prior to the pandemic, the nation-state was already re-emerging as a bulwark against the global market. Now the post-viral era has the potential to bring about a new settlement in which the protective state not only saves the economy but also strives more, at least in appearance, to serve the common good of society – beginning with greater national resilience concerning food, water, energy, medical supplies, manufacture and transportation.

But increased government intervention alone provides little more than a sticking plaster that leaves us vulnerable to the pandemics, ecological threats and social crises of the future. The reverse face of an expanded government role in the economy may be continued state support for the forces of unfettered capitalism and instrumental technology that already dominate and distort our daily lives. So far, tech platforms like Amazon, Google or China's Alibaba are the main winners of the impending economic depression, besides other corporate oligarchs that include newcomer Zoom. A system of bio-surveillance is taking shape with the power to monitor and manipulate the behaviour of whole populations. A postliberal protective state has to combine pluralist democracy with a corporatist conciliation of estranged interests and strong institutions that devolve power to people.

The third development is a stronger emphasis on bounded polities and national sovereignty. Free movement of capital has weakened the power of labour while the free movement of people without national economic development has put pressures on wages and hit workers. Bordered polities are an important condition for politicians to have the capacity to protect community and country. Nations represented democratically within sovereign states provide a vital source of legitimacy for government. But left unchecked, state sovereignty tends to slide into authoritarianism at home and anarchy abroad – as is prefigured in the works of Jean Bodin and Thomas Hobbes. That is why a postliberal politics seeks to hold in balance not just the central state and intermediary institutions but also patriotism and internationalism.

The fourth development is greater investment in public services and the role of civic community. Austerity, with its decimation of local government, has eroded the social fabric of Western countries, leaving them exposed to economic shocks and pandemics. The private sector is vital for prosperity based on investment and innovation, but it cannot replace the public provision of public goods that are irreducible to profit. That includes the need for strong civic institutions to uphold the ties of trust and cooperation. As the post-pandemic recovery unfolds, state and market risk reverting to the status quo ante – concentrating wealth and power in old elites or new classes who benefit from their preferred policy mix: technocratic 'global governance' that overrides democratic polities; cultural libertarianism that corrodes community and tradition; mass immigration and unfettered free trade that erode national industry, economic development and the social fabric. The postliberal alternative is to embed power and wealth in democratically governed institutions and strong social relations based on reciprocal obligations – the duties we owe one another.

What we are up against

What are the forces that a postliberal politics will have to contend with after the pandemic? Besides hostile foreign powers and tech totalitarianism, there are the forces of hyper-capitalism and extreme identity politics that disrupt the lives we assumed were solid. The plague exposes the frailty of human existence. This brings us back to Camus, who published *La peste* in 1947. One hundred years earlier, Karl Marx and Friedrich Engels wrote similarly about unprecedented disruption to settled ways of life: 'All that is solid melts into air, all that is holy is profaned, and man is at last compelled to face with sober senses his real conditions of life, and his relations with his kind.'[12]

The authors of the *Communist Manifesto* anticipated the coming age of modern globalization, with its first wave in the late nineteenth century, driven by a rapacious form of capitalism that recreated the world in its own image of relentless expansion: 'The need of a constantly expanding market for its products chases the bourgeoisie over the entire surface of the globe. It must nestle everywhere, settle everywhere, establish connexions everywhere.'[13] Marx and Engels opposed the emerging capitalist world, but they welcomed the destruction of the old order. Not unlike latter-day liberals, they assumed that reason, science and cosmopolitan values would fulfil the Enlightenment promise of progress.

Yet today hyper-capitalism has fused with extreme identity politics – whether the so-called 'Great Awokening' on the left or the alt-right that champions market nativism.[14] Together they erode trust, undermine institutions and trash our precious natural environment, destroying the basis of a common life shared across ages and classes. The Covid-19 pandemic could intensify these tendencies further, or it could inaugurate something more hopeful.

For Marxists, like liberals, historical progress is the ultimate morality that determines politics. Both are utopian visions with dystopian consequences – with all hope resting on human will, the forces of techno-science and the economy. Camus, by contrast, was keenly aware of the limits of determinism and utilitarian schemes of striving for the 'greatest happiness of the greatest number'. In Covid-19 times of utilitarian calculations about herd immunity, his words continue to serve as a cautionary note: '[E]veryone has it inside himself, this plague, because no one in the world, no one, is immune.'[15] It is a reminder about our fundamental vulnerability. Much of modern ideology turned abstract ideas into idols and sacrificed millions in the attempt to serve them. Going forward, politics has to start with our human and social condition of frailty – with people as they are in their families, localities and workplaces.

3

Why opposites coincide

In Dostoevsky's novel *Demons* (*Бесы* – *The Possessed* or *The Devils*, 1871), the revolutionary theorist Shigalyov devises a new social system using the tools of science to liberate people from the Tsarist tyranny. Yet by abandoning any ethical limits for the sake of untrammelled freedom, the politics that emerges is a type of tyranny more systematically violent than anything witnessed in the past. Shigalyov himself acknowledges the contradictory nature of his ideology: 'I have become entangled in my own data, and my conclusion stands in direct contradiction to the initial idea from which I started. Proceeding from unlimited freedom, I end with unlimited despotism.'[1]

Dostoevsky's dictum is doubly prophetic. He anticipated not only the twentieth-century descent of revolutionary liberation into totalitarian dictatorship but also the twenty-first-century slide of ultraliberal liberty into increasingly authoritarian control. This is best illustrated by the attack on free speech and pluralism, indulging in groupthink within 'safe spaces' to promote ideological uniformity, besides enhanced social engineering based on high-tech surveillance. But what Dostoevsky could not have foreseen is how authoritarian powers, chief of all China's current system, embrace liberal globalization and modern science to consolidate a digital police state. Western surveillance capitalism and China's tech totalitarianism are today's prime examples of Gramsci's 'morbid phenomena' in the interregnum – opposites that fraternize.

The great convergence

Liberalism and authoritarianism are the dominant ideologies of our age but neither is hegemonic. By exposing their shortcomings, the pandemic casts doubt on their legitimacy. Some Western liberals privileged the protection of the economy over the survival of persons most at risk – a radicalized utilitarian calculation that would have sacrificed the weakest in society. Others embraced total lockdown before abandoning it in favour of lawless protest in the wake of the George Floyd killing. While racism and police brutality need firm action, the tearing down of statues and the online censorship were an attack on the principles of liberality: free speech and free association. Meanwhile, authoritarians – from the US to Brazil, Eastern Europe, Russia and China – offered simplistic slogans and blamed foreign forces whereas countries need real leadership and international cooperation to be more resilient. Both worldviews promise a better future but are stuck in the past. They clamour for a return to the old normal of liberal technocracy or authoritarian demagogy – apparent opposites that end up converging and even coinciding.

This parallelism by no means entails moral equivalence. Liberalism and authoritarianism differ on fundamental principles and institutions such as freedom, equality, the rule of law or civil society. Nor does it equate all populist politics with authoritarian rule, an issue to which I shall revert in the following section. Nevertheless, *really existing* liberal and authoritarian models borrow from each other in ways that are complex and collusive.

Contemporary liberalism erodes the liberal tradition in two ways. First, it promotes ever-increasing negative liberty – freedom from restrictions except the law and private conscience – to the point where it flips over into the tyranny of individual choice abstracted from any relational constraints of family, community or nature. This can be termed ultraprogressivism, a blend of social egalitarianism, cultural individualism and market fundamentalism that has characterized both the centre-left and the centre-right since the 1990s. It radicalized the socially liberal turn of the left in the 1960s and the economically liberal turn of the right in the 1980s, culminating in their fusion in the late 1990s and early 2000s. At the heart of the ultraprogressivist creed lies the worship of individual autonomy, which is illiberal and authoritarian insofar as it marginalizes all those who desire greater communal solidarity.

Second, this form of liberalism has given rise to a phenomenon that in some sense is a backlash against it, but in another way intensifies its inner logic: identitarianism. It grows out of ultraprogressive identity politics and elevates all minority norms over majority interests. Identitarianism blends elements of revolutionary Marxist thought with cultural egalitarianism and strands in critical race, gender and queer theory, a toxic mix that corrodes free inquiry and free speech on university campuses and beyond.[2] Insofar as it opposes certain individual rights, identitarian ideology is deeply antiliberal. Worse, by radicalizing all aspects of social life in a Manichaean way, it slides into a fanaticism that is authoritarian and collectivist by pitting all the oppressed and exploited minorities against their supposedly racist oppressor majorities. It is both an extreme reaction against ultraprogressivism and a radicalization of its inner logic of opposing in-groups to out-groups with no possibility of a negotiated compromise. That is why the leadership of Black Lives Matter – with its encouragement of 'cancel culture' and its demand to erase all white privilege – is in some respects the mirror image of white supremacism. Older liberals either feel intimidated and are often too scared to oppose this antiliberal identity politics for fear of being branded racist or reactionary, or else they are lone voices who are abused on social media.[3]

Both ultraprogressives and identitarians threaten liberalism in the sense of a politics that endeavours to be generous and tolerant. Far from upholding tolerance and pluralism, they seek to enforce a single worldview based on fear and intimidation that ends with the despotism of mob rule. This outlook finds one of its most extreme expressions in so-called 'woke capitalism'.[4] It combines corporate crusades on progressive issues with the protection of monopolies in ways that fuse virtue signalling with naked self-interest. That is why the US economic establishment – Walmart, Facebook, Amazon, as well as Ivy League trustees and those in charge of the major sports leagues – supported the global protests against racism and funded Black Lives Matter, whose leadership is tainted by accusations of anti-Semitism.

Identitarians weaponize racial and other injustice to deploy new modes of social control, not least attempted bullying of the majority by way of riots, looting and frenzied acts of iconoclasm. Paradoxically, what started a century or so ago as the liberal struggle for equality dissolves into mob rule and mass lawlessness. There are multiple campaigns to rewrite school and university curricula, combined with attacks on any dissenters, who are hounded out of classrooms, workplaces and social media. The irony of imposing a uniform view about everything in the name of equality, diversity and inclusion seems lost on its advocates.

For their part, authoritarians in China and elsewhere fuse statist ideas with liberal hyper-globalization in a manner that atomizes society. The ensuing anarchy is used to legitimate ever-greater control of individuals, who are offered economic freedom in exchange for political oppression. The illusion of infinite consumer choice serves to conceal from view the erosion of political, civic and human rights. Citizenship and democracy are increasingly formal categories detached from a reality of authoritarian consolidation across society. Democratic rhetoric creates a spectacle of political competition where the outcome is predetermined by the dominant party or personal patronage – or both at once.[5] Rather than simply oppressing opposition parties, the ruling regime seeks to co-opt and corrupt any independent movements. Their continued existence legitimates the discourse about sovereign, managed democracy. Authoritarian leaders periodically invoke socially conservative values, but they fuse moral relativism with absolute political coercion and state capitalist economies. Economic liberalization, far from inaugurating greater political freedoms, has helped to consolidate centralized power. Liberal globalization will not democratize the likes of Russia or China but instead reinforce their totalitarian temptations – though this spectre haunts the latter far more than the former.

Dystopian dreams

Liberalism and authoritarianism not only converge on global capitalism or novel forms of social control. Both worldviews are also ugly utopias with dystopian consequences. They rest on the utilitarian promise of progress for the greatest number but, in reality, their attempt to restore prosperity and public health promotes a dystopia of disruptive technology and bio-surveillance that benefits a new professional-managerial class.

In the liberal West, this new class is composed of two 'castes'. First, there is an old elite and a new establishment that together form an oligarchy of finance and high tech exemplified by Wall Street and Silicon Valley. Oligarchs rule together with what the English poet and philosopher Samuel Taylor Coleridge called the clerisy, the second caste of professionals.[6] Today this takes the form of a sham clerisy who dominate much of the media, education and the civil service. 'The nexus between the clerisy and the oligarchy lies at the core of neo-feudalism,' argues the American writer Joel Kotkin, 'On the whole they share a common worldview and are allies on most issues.'[7] Both 'castes' are examples of how new classes radicalize certain trends in the old elites: the monopolizing tendencies of the corporate captains of industry and the cultural condescension on the part of the upper middle class.

These two castes are similar to the French economist Thomas Piketty's distinction between the Brahmin Left and the Merchant Right.[8] They represent, respectively, social progressives and economic liberals, but either way they do not trust the third estate: the 'people'. To these castes we must add a fourth, the legion of low-skilled migrant workers who form the urban outcasts in most

Western cities and who are joined in their precarious condition by growing numbers of the indigenous post-industrial working class and increasingly the lower middle class too.[9]

Distrust of the people is shared by authoritarian leaders. Such systems are plutocracies with two complementary classes. One is the class of oligarchs, who tend to dominate extractive industries and are part of power structures via a complex system of state banks and shadow banks.[10] China's Communist Party has created an entire edifice of crony capitalism built around a Red Nobility who amass billions even as their relatives are members of the Politburo pledging to be at the service of the people. The other is the class of 'political technologists', who are arguably the authoritarian equivalent of the West's sham clerisy. Political technology is a phenomenon that first emerged in 1990s post-Communist Russia to describe the use of both old and new media in military-style strategies of deception. To maintain a semblance of democracy, the ruling party combines top-down governance and practices of co-opting anti-regime actors with techniques taken from television, advertising, PR and increasingly the internet in order to generate a managed debate.[11]

In reality, oligarchs and political technologists conspire to control all forms of political discourse and prevent any independent movements from taking root. They also collude in exploiting both the class of people and the class of urban outcasts, who include those trapped in indentured labour, debt bondage or domestic servitude, which still exists in many places – including parts of the liberal West, where the scourge of modern slavery is bound up with the exploitative practices of global capitalism.[12]

Plutocracy and proletariat

The apparent opposites of liberalism and authoritarianism coincide in their erosion of both working and middle classes as well as the weakening of cross-class coalitions. In Western liberal democracies, the working classes have splintered into the precariat, the post-industrial working class and parts of the lower middle class. The middle classes are divided between the professional-managerial upper bourgeoisie and an increasingly proletarianized lower middle class that struggles to make ends meet. In authoritarian systems, the emergence of a new middle class is likely to go into reverse after the end of the pandemic as lower economic growth depresses both wages and house prices while state spending cannot compensate for the lack of private consumption.

The contemporary coincidence of opposites is possibly most striking in the US. It remains the world's first superpower in relation to economic wealth, military might, political influence, technological innovation and global cultural appeal. 'Yet at its centre,' writes the commentator Aris Roussinos, 'the US echoes post-Soviet Russia in its epidemics of death by drug overdose, in its collapsing middle class, its worsening health outcomes and declining life expectancies, the capture of the state and economy by rapacious oligarchs, and in the occasional bouts of interethnic violence leading to demonstrations, riots and broader political dysfunction.'[13] The 2020 protests and the storming of the Capitol on 6 January 2021 illustrate how America oscillates between anarchic release and coercive control.

Despite their differences, liberal and authoritarian ideologies end up converging around forms of capitalism that divide societies into plutocratic elites and a proletarianized populace – with the middle and working classes ever more eroded. Many people are resigned to a modicum of comfort and passive entertainment, together with routinized and uncreative work and poor prospects. Alongside the corrosion of character and the loss of older virtues of craftmanship, it leaves a feeling of uselessness among manual workers and younger professionals whose jobs are threatened by automation.[14] Without social recognition, national popular politics has unravelled, leaving a void filled by demagogues who are variously ultraprogressive or antiliberal.

Both worldviews claim to be on the 'right side of history' and put their faith in material progress, but neither anticipates the future with hope, thus precipitating a crisis of purpose and meaning. Starting with ultraprogressivism, its anthropological pessimism and superficial techno-optimism get reality the wrong way round. Humans are not by nature selfish, greedy, distrustful of others, prone to violence and in need of salvation based on the progress of science or technology. Instead, to recognize that humans are capable of virtue, not just vice, is to run with the grain of our nature, as the late philosopher Mary Midgley argued.[15] But for the very reason that humans are weak and prone to vice, we need to be sceptical about the power of science and technology in human hands.[16] This raises questions about both the material and ideational foundation of liberalism: the power of money and tech as well as the appeal to abstract ideals. The fusion of woke capitalism with extreme identity politics radicalizes contemporary liberalism to the point where it descends into an outright authoritarianism always lurking in the liberal logic.

Despotic demons

So besides capitalism, liberal and authoritarian ideologies also collaborate in creating a system of bio-surveillance in which the whole population is tracked and people's individual health conditions are centrally monitored all the time. It is not just intrusive online ads or gig workers under permanent pressure to get top ratings from their customers. Worse, tech platforms deploy new means of behaviour modification by mining data from the most intimate recesses of our selves which were once private. As personal experience is monetized in the interest of global capital, liberty turns into unfreedom. Technologies of monitoring and social control are able to manipulate us to the point where we freely yet unconsciously surrender our humanity to the clutches of surveillance capitalism – prisoners of the global online panopticon in which Facebook algorithms and Google's Artificial Intelligence know more about us than we do about ourselves.[17] It reflects the utilitarian philosopher Jeremy Bentham's utopian idea of the Panopticon: an ideal prison designed to keep inmates under permanent observation.

Bio-surveillance is the contemporary expression of a sacrificial utilitarian calculus that dispenses with the dignity of the person for the 'greater good' of the masses and their masters. China already deploys facial recognition technology that can detect elevated temperatures in a crowd or flag citizens who are not wearing a face mask. Another element of China's surveillance state is the social credit system: a government ranking of citizens' behaviour using both public and private data, which can strip people of rights and freedoms in case of non-compliance. The Chinese journalist Liu Hu, who writes about official corruption and censorship, found himself added to a 'List of Dishonest Persons Subject to Enforcement by the Supreme People's Court', which disqualified him from buying a plane ticket, booking certain trains, purchasing property or taking out a loan – without any evidence or trial. 'There was no file, no police warrant, no official advance notification. They just cut me off from the things I was once entitled to,' he says. 'What's really scary is there's nothing you can do about it. You can report to no one. You are stuck in the middle of nowhere.'[18]

Beijing's surveillance system is ultimately inspired by the French founding father of positivism Auguste Comte and his vision of a society in which humans are mechanical systems ruled by the laws of science. What matters is not the free choice of the individual but rather collective welfare, and this is best maximized by a class of technocratic planners and scientific elites who re-engineer human beings. It is that project built on inhuman methods of sacrificing weak members of society which Dostoevsky described as demonic. As with all utopian projects, today's revolutionaries have demons of their own. Possessed by fantastical ideas of ever-greater prosperity and public health, they end up inflicting misery and deadly viruses on people. It is not particular elites who are evil but certain ideas to which they are enslaved – such as the dangerous ideal of technologically enhanced humanity, ending in barbarism, or unfettered freedom, and leading inexorably and paradoxically to total tyranny.

4

New polarities

We owe the logic of left versus right to the French Revolution of 1789 and its rationalist, spatializing conception of politics.[1] Since history is contingent, there is nothing 'natural' or inevitable about this dualism. None of the totalitarian ideologies of the twentieth century fitted easily into left–right categories. Nor did the liberal turn of the left and the right from the 1960s to the 1990s. The dominance of liberalism is today being qualified by the intrusion of new polarities that cannot be conceptualized in binary terms either. These new polarities concern variously the globalist versus the nativist, the open society versus the closed society, the technocratic versus the populist, democracy versus authoritarianism and liberalism versus antiliberalism. In electoral terms, they seem to map neatly onto Remain/Leave in the Brexit referendum and Joe Biden against Donald Trump. Yet like liberalism, national populism does not coincide with the dichotomy of left versus right.[2]

Polar opposites do not tell the whole story, and the dualistic logic that underpins them conceals paradoxical combinations. After Brexit, the triumph of Trump and Boris Johnson's victory in the December 2019 general election, there was much talk about a fundamental realignment in Anglo-Saxon politics as the working classes abandoned the liberal left for national populists or one-nation conservatives who lean left on the economy and right on culture. Johnsonism, if such a thing exists, seems to be paradoxical rather than dualistic, combining an activist government that has ditched austerity for Keynesian state spending with a strong stance on law and order as well as greater limits on immigration.

Going left on the economy aims to unleash animal spirits and productivity in the hope of levelling up the 'left behind' parts of the country that supported Brexit, such as ex-Labour voters in Red Wall constituencies. Going right on culture seeks to shore up the Conservative base in the 'war on woke': the wave of activism that is attacking statues, memorials and free speech. Yet Johnson has not done much to defend the things that traditional conservatives care about: the family, community, morality in public life, cultural heritage or national identity.

Thus Johnson's politics could equally amount to a novel fusion of a mutated economic liberalism with elements of cultural antiliberalism. His government champions global trade deals and supports big business in the City of London. He and some of his advisers reject multiculturalism, dismiss the mainstream media, criticize judges and make disparaging comments about ethnic minorities. Such a mix is a contradiction in theory but may well be coherent in practice because it seems to forge an alliance of middle-class conservatives and blue-collar workers who are more united by their values than their economic interests. The assumption is that the new divide over values and identity cuts across the old divide over class and attitudes to the economy.[3]

New polarities

Is Johnson's brand of politics national-populist and antiliberal because it embraces the backlash against hyper-globalization with its deleterious effects such as deindustrialization, the mass mobility of people and a growing interdependence in relation to financial, environmental and viral risk? Or does he represent a realignment of Western politics in a postliberal, one-nation conservative direction of fusing greater economic radicalism with more social conservatism, reflecting a deeper shift of working-class support for the right and middle-class support for the left? National-populist or one-nation conservative? Antiliberal or postliberal?

That there is no simple answer to these questions suggests that our widest categories of political analysis are doubly inadequate and increasingly obsolete. First, they remain too confined to the old opposites of right versus left, which have to some extent been supplanted by a new polarity of liberal versus populist (or in some cases authoritarian). But second, even this simple polarity is woefully inadequate to understand what is now going on. For both the liberal and the populist camps are themselves bifurcated and sometimes act in complex collusion, as the previous section suggested. It is not just liberals who are profoundly divided between older liberals, on the one hand, and ultraprogressives and identitarians, whose politics is illiberal or even antiliberal, on the other hand.

There are divisions among populists too, notably between those who are nationalist, authoritarian and antiliberal and those who promote civic ties and patriotism in a more truly 'liberal' (because generous and tolerant) sense and are therefore closer to older liberals.[4] In this manner, the new polarity of liberal versus populist hides genuine alternatives. A truly postliberal

47

politics has to outflank both old opposites and new polarities in favour of a paradoxical position: economically radically yet socially moderate and ecologically balanced. Most people are broadly communitarian: small-c conservative in their approach to matters of state and small-s socialist on public services, fair play and hard work. They cherish liberty but value authority too.

The contradictions of right-wing postliberalism

There are groups of Conservatives or Republicans on either side of the Atlantic who seem postliberal to the extent that they reject free-market fundamentalism and the neoconservative foreign policy of permanent war. Yet apart from developing increasingly strident positions on international affairs and immigration policy, these groups have little to offer other than opposing globalism in the name of nationalism. One prominent example in the US is the group behind 'National Conservatism', an initiative by the Israeli intellectual Yoram Hazony, who argues that nations are in perpetual and diametric opposition to empires – even though this ignores the history of England and America.[5] What may look postliberal turns out to be mostly antiliberal.

Other right-wing postliberals reject nationalism and seek to develop a patriotic agenda for both the domestic economy and foreign policy. Examples include Senators such as Marco Rubio and analysts like Oren Cass, who argues that labour markets in which workers cannot support strong families and communities are incompatible not just with conservatism but also with the goal of long-term prosperity.[6] These figures also agree on bolstering law and order through a combination of shorter and longer custodial sentences, though prisoner rehabilitation and more equal access to justice based on better funded legal aid are missing from their policies. Clamping down on immigration will satisfy popular demands for greater security but not reverse social fragmentation or address community breakdown.

The fundamental dividing line between right-wing antiliberals and postliberals is capitalism. The former back big business and some of them seek to unleash the forces of technology and accelerated capitalism. How their revolutionary reforms will foster social stability and a greater sense of belonging is unclear. Insofar as the right struggles to conceptualize capitalism as a force of dispossession with its deep roots in liberal thought, it will not be able to imagine a postliberal politics. As the late conservative philosopher Roger Scruton reminded the post-Thatcher Tory Party, the unfettered market turns everyone and everything into a commodity, leaving us atomized and alienated.[7]

Others on the right profess to uphold the social justice tradition of the churches while advocating central state power to replace compassion for people in need with draconian social control. This includes Conservative or Republican support for welfare rationalization to the point where people who care for relatives end up losing their benefits. It treats human beings like administrative units whose contribution to community and country is deemed worthless. They get 'nothing for something'. For the political right, such people are either inevitable sacrifices to the liberal market, or else they are a bunch of lazy misfits who need to be disciplined by the authoritarian state, or both at once.

In truth, most contemporary Republicans and Tories are not compassionate conservatives or even conservatives. At their hands, the rhetoric of one-nation or national conservatism is a cipher for the free-market fundamentalism of regulatory divergence and global trade deals, combined with social regression and culture wars. What may look postliberal turns out to be a combination of the old and the new right orthodoxies and so is doubly wrong. This is what the populist and now post-pandemic moment brings to the fore. Consider the Brazilian leader Jair Bolsonaro, who, rather like Trump, combines elements of economic libertarianism with nationalist undertones or even atavistic ethno-centrism.

This may sound antiliberal, but in reality it reinforces a certain underlying liberal logic. First, there is the unmediated will of the individual (Hobbes) or the masses (Rousseau) – or both at once. Second, there is the subordination of any substantive notion of the common good to individual freedoms (Locke) or collective material utility (Bentham) – or again both at once. We have come full circle from liberalism to distorted forms of postliberalism that are at once ultraliberal in economic terms and antiliberal in social terms. Opposites coincide and define a political space that excludes paradoxical combinations: the bio-conservationist versus the transhuman, rootedness versus mobility, the interpersonal versus the anonymous, the virtuous versus the amoral and, indeed, the postliberal versus the ultraliberal and the antiliberal.

Making sense of politics

A sophisticated political analysis needs now to be quadrilateral: not left versus right or liberal versus populist or libertarian versus authoritarian, but rather the axes of communitarian as opposed to individualist/

collectivist and pluralist and corporatist as opposed to statist/capitalist. That is because individualism and collectivism as well as statism and capitalism are but two sides of the same coin: unfettered individualism dissolves into mass lawlessness, mob rule and collectivist power, while free-market fundamentalism either relies on state coercion for its ever-greater expansion into all areas of social life or leads to variants of state capitalism. By contrast, a communitarian and pluralist politics avoids these extremes in favour of the dignity of the person, intermediary institutions and the reality that we are bound by bonds of reciprocity.

The appeal of populism and authoritarianism is not limited to certain postliberal intellectuals. Today the excluded majority may readily fall prey to unmediated democratic aggregation and control by a seemingly benign centre and the rule of a strong man. But it is far from clear that most populists or authoritarians are communitarians at all: to the contrary, the evidence from Brazil and elsewhere is that they are sometimes happy to embrace a 'Protestant' promise of success to the individually hard-working (supported by the Charismatic 'prosperity gospel') alongside state-backed discriminations, rationalized welfare and an authoritarian state.

There is also much evidence that many within the excluded majority (and even considerable numbers of the foot-soldiers of the elites in the citadels)[8] are looking for a combination that is not as yet on offer from any political party anywhere: greater economic equality combined with moderate social stability that is pro-family, combined with a respect for tradition, belonging and place in both cultural and ecological senses. That is the mode of postliberalism which this book develops.

To conclude the first part of this book: our future could be determined by a sheer endless cycle of hyper-capitalism and its periodic crises and popular backlashes against extreme identity politics of the far left or the radical right. In addition, we might witness a resumption of the battle between these two dominant tendencies more akin to the resumption of unqualified liberal imperialism versus militaristic nationalism that ensued upon the ending of the First World War.[9] Yet the pandemic also offers a historic chance to build a new consensus that is truly postliberal: a paradoxical politics of the common good that safeguards the liberal principles of freedom and equality by injecting social solidarity into the body politic. After the pandemic and the protests, there is a realization that liberalism and authoritarianism are failing, but not yet a public political philosophy of postliberalism.

II

A PUBLIC PHILOSOPHY OF POSTLIBERALISM

Purpose, hope and dignity are some of the principles that define a public philosophy of postliberalism. It brings together a number of philosophical traditions, such as virtue ethics, Renaissance humanism, Romanticism, personalism, pluralism and certain elements of communitarianism. Common to these very diverse traditions is the idea that politics is not a utilitarian science of maximizing the happiness of the greatest number but rather a practice of ethical judgement for the flourishing of all persons as they are in their families, localities and workplaces. At the heart of postliberal philosophy is the primacy of the human and the interpersonal, which are more fundamental than the impersonal forces of power, wealth and technology, combined with a respect for inheritance and belonging in both cultural and ecological senses.

It is love for what the French philosopher Simone Weil calls 'rootedness': 'the real, active and natural participation in the life of the community which preserves in living shape certain particular treasures of the past and certain particular expectations for the future'.[1] It might be the satisfaction of the Christian participating in the ancient liturgy and sacraments of the Church (or indeed, more prosaically, the annual parish festival); of keeping your local pool or darts team at your sports and social club going; or of campaigning to keep your football team from becoming the plaything of another foreign oligarch. As Weil wrote in 1943 in her 'Draft for a Statement of Human Obligations', 'The human soul needs above all to be rooted in several natural environments and to make contact with the universe through them.' Tracing a social philosophy back to Antiquity and early Christianity, for her this environment includes 'a man's country, and places where his language is spoken, and places with a culture or historical past which he shares, and his professional milieu, and his neighbourhood'.[2]

5

The art of politics

'Following the science' is an odd strategy for a government whose mandate rests on the pledge to 'take back control'. Especially in an epidemiological emergency, politics cannot be about facts as if they were somehow more fundamental than values. It is about decision allied to judgement about ethical choices. When Covid-19 was first declared a pandemic, the political and moral questions focused on the relative virtues of herd immunity versus suppressing the viral spread and of sustaining the economy versus protecting immediately threatened lives. The natural sciences have no comprehensive answer to these questions, nor does political science modelled on physical laws and underpinned by instrumental rationality.

Responding to these questions is a matter not for abstract theory but for ethics and politics defined as a set of practices embedded in the relationships and institutions of a bounded polity. It is what Aristotle terms a *praxis*. Politics, if it is to have an ethical outlook and not be amoral or outrightly corrupt, needs to be aligned with human and social activity – not abstract utopias or sectional interests. For Aristotle, like his teacher Plato, political practice involves both *epistêmê* and *technê* in the sense of theoretical knowledge and practical art or craft. Along with a sense of statecraft, much of the contemporary West has abandoned foundational principles of politics and embraced instead short-term economic expediency. The US and UK in particular have outsourced the production of necessities to the sweat-shops of the world in China and relied on importing critical health equipment made by forced Uighur labour overseen by the Chinese Communist Party. The collusion of capitalism and communism is another instance of how apparent opposites coincide.[1] First economics and then politics have neglected their roots in moral philosophy, and it is time to re-moralize both.

Governance by number

Science plays a key role in advising politicians, but it cannot replace ethical discernment or political decision. The condition of political leaders being able to decide in time is a function of sovereign power, which – *pace* the German jurist Carl Schmitt – does not boil down to declaring the state of emergency but rather consists in upholding the conditions for human flourishing of a people within a defined polity. 'Following the science' means not just that the ground rules of everyday conduct are henceforth determined predominantly by scientific evidence derived from data and modelling. It also implies that the foundations of political authority are not to be found in the *demos* and its capacity for democratic self-government – Abraham Lincoln's ideal of 'government of the people, by the people, for the people'.

Instead, political authority is now redefined by what the French social theorist Alain Supiot calls 'governance by number'.[2] This cybernetic vision imagines a world in which social harmony can be founded on measurement. Far from reflecting the reality of messy social relations, laws and rules based on scientific evidence are seen as the most efficient means by which society can attain quantifiable ends like economic growth or individual happiness. 'Everything can be measured, and what gets measured gets managed', as the motto of the management consultancy McKinsey goes. Governance by number extends this from the sphere of economics to the realm of politics and social life. Such a conception fundamentally changes the nature of politics as praxis. If, as the Prussian general and military theorist Carl von Clausewitz put it, 'war is the continuation of politics by other means', politics is now the extension of economics by scientific means.

This underpins much of the influential Chicago School of economics, which helped to establish the neoliberal creed on which the centrist consensus of the last four decades was built. Chicago economists effectively equate all economic agents with utilitarian calculators. In his 1956 book *Money, Interest and Prices*, the economist Don Patinkin anticipated this view: 'We can consider the individual – with his given indifference map and initial endowment – to be a "utility computer" into whom we "feed" a sequence of market prices and from whom we obtain a corresponding sequence of "solutions" in the form of specified optimum positions.'[3] This extends the calculation of utility to the public sector and the private sphere, thereby economizing the entire social reality.

Using the mindless mantra of 'modernization', successive governments – from the Clinton Democrats and New Labour to George W. Bush's Republicans and the Conservative/LibDem coalition – invoked efficiency and 'value for money' even as they wasted billions on public procurement from private oligopolies. Just as twentieth-century communism replaced the government of the people with the administration of things, so now twenty-first-century capitalism replaces both with the management of units – governance by number. Larry Summers, a Harvard economist who played a leading role in the Clinton and Obama administrations, has said that 'the laws of economics are like the laws of engineering. One set of laws works everywhere'[4] – and presumably always.

Politics as an economistic science is devoid of ethics, with the ensuing moral vacuum being filled by a combination of liberal legalism and Benthamite utilitarian calculation. For legalists like John Rawls or Ronald Dworkin, law is a repository of moral truth, which can be codified beyond reasonable doubt. For utilitarian thinkers like Jeremy Bentham and his contemporary followers, life as the maximizing of pleasure and the minimizing of pain implies that we can measure what is valuable. This fallacy equally applies to GDP, which fails to count unpaid work, all manner of relational goods and the shadow economy.[5] Taken together, laws and rules at the service of the 'greatest happiness of the greatest number' are less to do with the just ordering of a polity than with an experiment in large-scale social engineering: turning us all into utility-maximizing agents. Along with the extension of rights and entitlements into all spheres of life, the calculus of individual happiness or general welfare has hollowed out politics and redefined what makes us human: our capacity for maximum free choice in the economy is now assumed to override our social, political nature and our quest for both individual fulfilment and mutual flourishing.

Libertarian paternalism

Behavioural science, in part drawing on moral psychology, takes this to the next level. Of course, events such as the pandemic necessitate a change in behaviour: 'staying at home' during the lockdown or 'staying alert' as restrictions are eased. To the extent that behavioural science incorporates moral instincts such as saving lives even at the expense of utility, it allows for a richer conception of politics. But it nonetheless reduces human nature to a set of individual psychological dispositions that are considered to be more fundamental than any mutual moral sentiment such as sympathy or fellow-feeling, of which Queen Elizabeth II spoke in her address to the nation in April 2020:

> I hope in the years to come everyone will be able to take pride in how they responded to this challenge. And those who come after us will say that the Britons of this generation were as strong as any. That the attributes of self-discipline, of quiet good-humoured resolve and of fellow-feeling still characterise this country. The pride in who we are is not a part of our past, it defines our present and our future.[6]

To ignore bonds of reciprocity diminishes politics by equating public morality with private psychology, which behavioural sciences draw on to propose an approach known as 'nudge': the idea of positive inducements or stimuli to influence individual or group behaviour.[7] At the heart of nudge is the idea of 'libertarian paternalism', which aims simultaneously to boost and constrain free choice. Yet far from promoting true social freedom that is mindful of self-restraint, nudge

59

rests on a deterministic conception of human nature. People cannot be trusted to make the right decisions for themselves, which opens the door for much more forceful intervention in the name of free choice. As the political theorist William Davies has argued, 'there is something nihilistic about a world-view that reduces morality to a type of predictable behavioural reaction. Rules lose their sense of rightness, and become instead a pure instrument to alter what someone is doing.'[8] Behind the language of incentives and rewards for responsible behaviour lies subtle, potentially sinister manipulation.

The fundamental problem with this approach is twofold: first of all, that it considers formal rules to be more fundamental than informal norms and, second, that the purpose of politics is supposedly to impose rules rather than reflect norms. This is surely shown in the often incredibly rigid way that pandemic instructions were enacted, with little room for common sense or adapting the spirit of the rules to individual situations. Politics as the enforcing of rules divorced from norms becomes increasingly arbitrary and unjust. If rules are purely self-referential, then they reflect the power of rule-makers. While rules and laws have exceptions, they depend for their legitimacy on being universally valid and being applied consistently. The reason for the fury over Boris Johnson's former adviser Dominic Cummings driving 30 miles during lockdown to 'test his eyesight' was his sense of entitlement to be exempt from the very government rules that he had helped to design. It violated norms of fair play and shared sacrifice. Along with the cover provided by the Prime Minister, Cummings' lack of contrition and shame reinforced the impression that the powerful can dispense with honour and humility.

Good government, good life

If rules reflect common norms embedded in customs and mores, then they go beyond prescribed behaviour or sanctions. As Davies points out, they involve a shared sense of mutual obligation to uphold them. Such an obligation is not reducible to the private conscience of individuals but extends to social relations and the covenantal ties between the generations. Without a sense of reciprocal obligation, society slides into a state of disorder that requires ever-greater surveillance and coercion. Machiavelli's Prince and Hobbes' Leviathan involve popular consent but both models of politics are ultimately based on sovereign power that rides roughshod over customs and norms.

In the Western tradition, the Machiavellian-Hobbesian account departs fundamentally from the Aristotelian-Thomist conception of politics as an art of persuasion and good government, which rests on an idea of right reason in search of ethical ends such as the good life. Versions of this ideal can be found in almost all political traditions: from Renaissance humanism to Romanticism, from personalism to pluralism, from one-nation conservatism to ethical socialism and from strands of classical liberalism to the new liberalism of T.H. Green, J.A. Hobson and L.T. Hobhouse.[9]

The idea of the good life is not grounded in some abstract utopian order or an authority beyond the rule of law. Rather, the good life emerges from the everyday experience of individuals and communities with different values who try to live together peaceably. But value pluralism and peaceful co-existence are only possible within a shared polity that is committed to the common good: the individual fulfilment and mutual

61

flourishing of all persons. Otherwise plural values will dissolve as political tribes clash and a revived social Darwinism takes hold once again.

Fundamental to our quest for the common good are democracy and pluralism: the peaceful resolution of conflict based on a plural search for truth anchored in mutual education. Yet today, democratic politics and pluralist societies are under threat from capitalism, technology, hostile foreign powers and the interplay of technocracy with demagogy at home. The promise of progress after 1989 has given way to regressive forces that fuel economic inequalities, ecological devastation, military adventurism and the decline of social cohesion. The catastrophic Covid-19 crisis has laid bare the erosion of our structures of common existence, while the deep desire for community that a majority of people expressed through generous acts of social solidarity is yet to be represented by any political party or government. A vision of the good life and reciprocal flourishing is a goal that is as compelling as it is elusive.

Driven by social media outrage and an economy of attention, public debate is shifting from reasonable discussion and respectful argument to a cacophony of condemnation and online abuse.[10] Both the revolutionary left and the radical right display moral self-righteousness while engaging in vicious campaigns of 'cancel culture' and demonization – silencing critics and even erasing historical memory. Free speech and our cultural inheritance are on the line. Our age of polarization is openly hostile to the democratic and pluralist conditions for the good life. As John Gray has argued in the wake of the pandemic and the protests, 'the task is maintaining a fragile peace in a culture of fragments. We are going to have to learn how to live with disorder, just as we must learn to live with the virus.'[11]

An appeal to common values will not temper tensions or resolve conflicts precisely because incommensurable norms drive the many divisions within contemporary societies – young and old, university educated or not, city and town – which align with the political polar opposites of Remain and Leave or Biden and Trump. It seems that the values divide underpinning the opposition between liberalism and authoritarianism – with populism somewhere on the spectrum – rules out any real prospect for a politics of the good life. In times of 'culture wars' and political polarization, appeals to a sphere of shared meaning seem to ring hollow.

Yet the desire for a meaningful life is inscribed into our human nature and instilled by our cultural inheritance – however much it may be contested. A quest for meaning combines the precious gifts of liberty and equality with a sense of self-restraint and solidarity. As Mary Harrington and the late Wendy Wheeler put it at the 2019 Windsor symposium, the bonds of family and friends, the givenness of our biological selves, the constraints of law, custom and faith, as well as our obligations to one another, all confer limits on personal autonomy. But they are also rich sources of relational meaning and dignity. A plural search for shared meaning defines the space for postliberal politics.

So even in times of social fragmentation and political polarization, the good life is a realistic ideal because it reflects the popular desire for an ordering of relationships that holds individual fulfilment in balance with mutual flourishing. My well-being is inextricably intertwined with yours, just like the equality of all depends on the dignified treatment of each.

This is only unrealistic as long as we remain wedded to the dominant assumptions. If, however, we embrace the actually realistic perspective of mutual benefit, then the public realm is conceivably able to tolerate legitimate moral differences and will not turn them into conflicts which can no longer be settled by reasonable compromise. All this requires good government and a politics that starts with shared interests rather than divisive values.

Conciliation of interests

Such a politics is what the English political theorist Bernard Crick calls the conciliation of rival interests in a polity using compromise rather than force. Crick's conception of politics shifts the focus away from abstractions and ideologies towards the praxis of 'preserving a community' that has 'grown too complicated for either tradition alone or pure arbitrary rule to preserve it without the undue use of coercion'. [12] Two conditions are necessary for a practice of political conciliation: the first condition is the existence of pluralistic societies that are culturally complex and in which values divide people, which is captured well by John Gray's notion of 'a culture of fragments'; the second condition is a commitment to rule out the use of force in settling conflicts, which applies to functioning democracies. In the words of Crick, to conceptualize politics in this manner 'is to assert, historically, that there are some societies at least which contain a variety of different interests and different moral viewpoints and [also] to assert, ethically, that conciliation is at least to be preferred to coercion among normal people'.[13]

Key to Crick's account is the recognition that diversity of interests and ethical values is itself a good and that therefore politics cannot be about the imposition of a single truth or set of absolute truths, for that would amount to tyranny. Nor can politics deny any sense of truth altogether, for that would lead to anarchy. In between those extremes that fuel each other, the vocation of politics is to represent 'at least some tolerance of different truths, some recognition that government is possible, indeed best conducted, amid the open canvassing of rival interests [...] that type of government where politics proves successful in ensuring reasonable stability and order'.[14] Survival and security are the common interests holding disparate groups together, not 'some allegedly objective "general will" or "public interest"'.[15]

It is here that Crick makes the decisive argument about the nature of politics: that there are no absolutely rational or scientific ways of resolving conflicts between incommensurable values or even rival interests. The reverse side of a rational objective order that has supposedly universal validity is the other contemporary tendency of reducing all moral judgements to expression of personal preferences based on subjective emotions.[16] As rationalism and emotivism dominate discourse, politics as the pursuit of ethical ends shrivels away. Therefore, politics has to transcend both science and sentimentality in the direction of what Aristotle calls *phronêsis* or practical wisdom, by which he means linking our ethical dispositions to the right course of action: the search for the good in everything we do.

Politics as the art of the actual

Such a conception of politics can be found in the works of Edmund Burke, notably his notion of 'principled practice', which means striving for a middle path between mere facts without ideas and pure abstraction without practical meaning. Burke's characterization of what distinguishes a statesman from a politician illustrates this well: 'A statesman, never losing sight of principles, is to be guided by circumstances' and 'A statesman forms the best judgement of all moral disquisitions who has the greatest number and variety of considerations in one before him, and can take them in with the best possible consideration of the middle result of them.'[17] In our age of polarization, Aristotle's and Burke's injunction of a middle path is not nostalgia for a moderate centrism that has long collapsed. Rather, it is a radical centre above and beyond the extremes of what Michael Lind calls technocratic neoliberalism and demagogic populism.[18]

Politics is often referred to as the art of the possible, but the category of possibility belongs much more to natural science with its focus on modelling and probability. Politics is not the science of the possible, but the art of the actual. It has to begin with how the world is and then chart a path towards the good life for all. That might seem far too idealistic, but it reflects realistic expectations. In the 1970s, Norman Kirk, the former Prime Minister of New Zealand, famously said that people do not want much. They want 'someone to love, somewhere to live, somewhere to work and something to hope for'. It may sound a little trite, but it contains a grain of truth. Love, home, work and hope as the building blocks for the good life. Relationships and a sense of belonging. A home that provides shelter and emotional stability. A job that offers us income and meaning. And a sense of hopefulness that life will improve for us and our loved ones.

But what do love, home, work, and hope mean in societies which face economic and cultural insecurity as well as levels of uncertainty unseen since the two world wars? As John Kay and Mervyn King argue, since uncertainty is a fundamental reality of both the economy and social life, policy-makers – and political leaders – need narratives to make sense of numbers.[19] Amid all the white noise of algorithm-engineered data, good decision-making requires a conceptual story. Transformative policies depend on the persuasive power of the underlying narrative. Here as elsewhere, judgement is key as it enables informed decisions about which models or sets of data to follow based on both history and theory. Otherwise governance by number slides into government by algorithm – with the chaotic consequences on display in the A-levels fiasco of August 2020.

Linked to judgement is leadership, taking brave decisions and leading from the front – not from behind, as Barack Obama seemed to suggest. In an emergency like Covid-19, simply 'following the science' amounts to an abdication of responsibility. It is not what Boris Johnson's hero Winston Churchill would have done. In the critical moments of the Second World War, Churchill argued that 'at the summit, true politics and strategy are one'. He challenged the generals and, when the national destiny warranted it, overruled them, whereas Johnson first ignored warning signals from countries such as Italy and then reluctantly agreed to the lockdown too late – thrice: in March 2020, in November 2020 and in January 2021. But it is not just about the Prime Minister and his former chief strategist. The UK – and, for that matter, the US – came up short. Weak state capacity and some poor advice from scientific and other senior advisers were not corrected by political judgement. And political weakness and a lack of leadership were not corrected by strong institutions.

In times of coronavirus, it is easy to vacillate between optimism that 'things can only get better' and pessimism that nothing will ever change. Just as the Covid-19 pandemic has laid bare the weakness of social relationships and institutions, so too it reveals the deep desire for communal solidarity. The art of politics is to reflect this reality and build plural spaces in which people can pursue the good life. Giving people a share in those things that make life worth living requires political imagination and courage, both of which are currently in short supply.

6

Social virtues

Fortitude, loyalty, generosity and other social virtues are largely absent from contemporary political discussion. In the West, politics revolves around a dichotomy of technocratic facts versus partisan values that reflects both Comtean positivism and the Weberian fusion of bureaucracy with charismatic leadership (but in today's political classes, the latter is sorely lacking in gravitas). The right's obsession with liberty *qua* free choice is as arbitrary as the left's pursuit of equality *qua* sameness is abstract. The right champions freedom and equal opportunity as an expression of its belief in the individual and self-advancement, whereas the left speaks the language of social justice and morality as an expression of its belief in collective fairness and progress. Both seek to bend the arc of history in their own direction and they end up converging towards a Whig history of faith in the forces of modernity – in particular capitalism and technocracy, but also an aggressive secularism that strips the sacred from our public square.

A public philosophy of postliberalism

Value pluralism

Values of free choice and abstract equality have become reified and disconnected from the everyday experience of ordinary people. For values to unify divided societies, they require a shared moral horizon – some common set of coordinates by which a society can navigate conflicts. Building on the agonistic liberalism of Isaiah Berlin, John Gray argues that 'political life, like moral life, abounds in radical choices between rival goods and rival evils, where reason leaves us in the lurch and whatever is done involves loss and sometimes tragedy'.[1] Along with the loss of cherished traditions, grief has become privatized as our politics and the public realm are increasingly sanitized. Discussion seems to veer from moral righteousness to technocratic administration with little sense of collective memory or shared cultural customs.

But in a context of value pluralism, how can societies try to resolve a clash of rival rights or conflicting principles? Feminism versus transgender rights, autonomy versus restraint, individual choice versus social cohesion are just some of the seemingly irreconcilable conflicts. Reconciling these differences cannot be limited to the application of reason alone but has to involve feeling and habit embedded in shared social practices. Despite our fragmented societies, there are still some social practices binding people together, such as sport, music, religious worship or having a drink down the pub. Football and the local club are good examples. They are both symbols of local pride and real communities of belonging that provide an anchor to people's existence. The former Liverpool manager Bill Shankly was only half joking when he said that 'Some people think football is a matter of life and death. I assure you, it's much more serious than that.' For millions of people past and present football represents a deeper part of who they are and where they come from. Love of sport expresses a moral sentiment no less important than our faculty of reasoning.

Moral sentiments are a matter of dispositions that are deeply engrained in cultures and the character of their peoples. As the academic Jonathan Rutherford has remarked, Britain is both conservative and radical in its sentiment, and arguably other Western countries are too.[2] These dispositions, as he argues, are not ideological or party political. They are qualities of mind and character that are woven into the fabric of national cultures. Radicals call for the transformation of injustice, tackling oppression and exploitation and giving people a sense of agency. Conservatives believe in inherited authority and traditions as sources of meaning and purpose. A proper balance of radical with small-c conservative dispositions is key to nurturing relationships and building institutions for a more just ordering of common life in society.

But when a country's cultural fabric unravels and a shared moral horizon disappears, are we not left only with some basic values on which to build a common political life? Do not the values of democracy, human rights and the rule of law provide what the philosopher John Rawls calls the foundations for an 'overlapping consensus': the way proponents of rival moral doctrines can agree on principles of fairness on which to base a polity with its social institutions?[3] In a 'culture of fragments' (John Gray), what else is left to salvage democracy? Yet as the philosopher Alasdair MacIntyre argued in his seminal book *After Virtue*, it is precisely such a shared standard that the dominant values of

Enlightenment modernity rule out because they assume the primacy of the individual and her or his will over the common good. Therefore the good ceases to be a transcendent horizon towards which human actions are ordered.[4]

Enlightenment values have replaced the good with individual rights devoid of equally robust obligations. They have replaced a covenant between generations and groups within the body politic (Burke's partnership between 'those who are living, those who are dead and those who are to be born') with a social contract among individuals who are assumed originally to be asocial and apolitical.[5] And they have replaced the practice of virtues, such as courage or practical wisdom, with an appeal to foundational values such as 'life, liberty and the pursuit of happiness' or *liberté, égalité* and *fraternité*. The difference between virtues and values is that virtues are embedded in practices and embodied in relationships and institutions, whereas values are often abstract and removed from the common life of people. Virtue provides a way of finding commonality while accommodating differences because it expresses ends that are social, not individual.

Ancient virtues renewed

Today it seems that we are stuck with abstract values, lacking the educative processes and institutional support for nurturing virtuous behaviour. More than seventy-five years ago, the writer Lewis Mumford made this point well:

> Virtue is not a chemical product, as Taine once described it: it is a historic product, like language and literature; and this means that if we cease to care about it, cease to

cultivate it, cease to transmit its funded values, a large part of it will become meaningless, like a dead language to which we have lost the key.[6]

Without some shared understanding of the good, what can societies do? Contemporary culture is fundamentally fragmented, as Gray says, but political communities can try to build a common life if they discover shared interests combined with the social virtues inscribed into our human nature: mutual dependency, association, self-organization, community, attachment and affection.

Individuals with radically different values can agree on the importance of dependency upon others and the need for human association. There is no good life without free and democratically self-governing associations that respect the rule of law, such as trade unions, universities, faith communities, charities, sport clubs and the entire edifice of civic institutions. Yes, the proportion of people joining local organizations or volunteering has sharply declined in recent decades.[7] It is equally true that online groups are a poor substitute as no amount of screen time can replace relationships with people in the places where they live. Yet Covid-19 has revealed the extraordinary capacity of human beings to forge new ties using technology as well as to rediscover neighbourhoods and the local community.[8] The outpouring of solidarity was an expression of a natural instinct of fraternal love that runs with the grain of our humanity.

Living a meaningful existence requires a measure of social order and security, protecting people from chaos and violence while at the same time creating spaces for self-organization and transformative change. Love and relationships need communal institutions, from the family to the workplace and from the neighbourhood to the nation. And identities are only distinct and stable insofar as they belong to a common culture, which grows out of inherited traditions of language, music, sport, food and fashion, alongside national institutions of popular attachment and affection such as parliaments, national churches or the armed forces. That is why the attack on the Capitol by a riotous mob of Trump supporters in January 2021 provoked revulsion across the political divide.

In politics, as in society, it is the social virtues of kindness, humility and mercy that help to sustain relationships and institutions. As Erasmus of Rotterdam put it, the character traits in political leaders which are 'farthest removed from tyranny' are the qualities of 'clemency, affability, fairness, courtesy and kindliness'. Other desirable dispositions include 'integrity, self-restraint, seriousness and alertness'.[9] The list of social virtues goes on. But in a context of value pluralism, can societies agree on a number of shared virtues or even a common conception of virtue? Greco-Roman philosophy, one of the pillars of Western civilization, has bequeathed to us four perennial principles. In the words of Cicero, 'virtue may be defined as a habit of mind in harmony with reason and the order of nature. It has four parts: prudence, justice, temperance and courage.'[10] Prudence is about the careful pursuit of practical wisdom beyond mere opinion and technical knowledge. Justice seeks to bring about a fair ordering of relations within the polity. Temperance calls us to restraint or self-control in an attempt to limit the vices of greed or lust. And courage is the fortitude and ability to confront fear without cowardice or recklessness. But our late modern or postmodern culture rules out of the court of public discussion any notion of an 'order of nature'. Without such an order and without a shared standard of rationality, any appeal to the four classical virtues seems hollow.

Yet social virtues are dispositions or habits of the mind, ingrained in human nature, in competition with vices and variously encouraged or distorted by cultural practices. Honour is a universal principle, but 'honour killings' are an extreme perversion of it. All cultures depend on translating certain principles into rules of social practices. Often cultures confuse practices with principles to the point where criticism of a certain practice is taken as an attack on the principle which it is supposed to embody. But tolerance and pluralism imply respect for other people's principles and commitments, without necessarily implying that a particular practice should be condoned. A practice can therefore be seen as a cultural expression of a principle. Particular practices reflect specific cultural conceptions of a universal principle that is embodied in them. One example, linked to the virtue of temperance, is the practice of moderate drinking within most families and communities as part of a culture of limits and mutual regard. The stark contrast with many city-centre bars with their promotions of cheap strong drinks relates to a culture of bacchanalian excess and the absence of communal considerations. It is a matter of how universal principles of relationality or individualism shape particular practices.

In the West, the main tradition that has transformed our understanding of the four classical virtues is Christianity. The theological virtues of faith, hope and charity are more democratic because everyone can exercise them – notably the universal virtue of love. This is fundamentally different from Homer's idealization of military prowess or Aristotle's prioritization of the aristocracy. And as Krzysztof Kieślowski's film *Blue*

A public philosophy of postliberalism

suggests, the Enlightenment values of liberty, equality
and fraternity, if they are to avert irreconcilable contradictions, need an injection of faith, hope and love. The
pursuit of justice requires belief – or a 'leap of faith'
– in the possibility that justice can be done, just as
the commitment to the dignity of each person and the
equality of all people involves hope that humans can
limit their propensity to vice and increase their practice
of virtue. Faith in the sense of trust (*pistis*, in Plato) is
the belief that human beings are capable of love in their
relationships and that compassion and charity can be
instilled in social behaviour and even institutions.

A shared moral horizon

Our age of polarization seems hostile to any common
conception of the good. Nor does our dominant culture
appear to value virtue. To quote MacIntyre again, the
key question is this: 'are there too many different and
incompatible conceptions of virtue, for there to be any
real unity to the concept or indeed to the history?'[11] It
seems that we face not only *value* pluralism but also
virtue pluralism. Yet beyond the undeniable reality
of rival virtues that clash (prudence versus justice
or temperance versus courage), there is an equally
undeniable reality of human wrongs that are recognized within and across different cultures: betrayal,
humiliation, torture, unlawful imprisonment, slavery,
tyranny and other human wrongs that are either
outlawed or viewed as moral taboos. Like human
rights, the recognized existence of human wrongs
implies that cultural and civilizational traditions share
certain ethical principles which are seen as universal.
One indication is the length to which people and

governments around the world go in trying to cover up crimes for fear of being found out and confronted by truths that go against long-established norms. And then there is the self-deception involved in committing human wrongs. Mary Midgley calls this the 'special lies that people tell themselves and each other to justify doing unjustifiable things'.[12]

Like social virtues, human wrongs evolve. Practices change, even if principles are perennial and endure. Abolishing slavery and outlawing torture are just two examples where a perverted practice was finally classified as a crime, even if this has not prevented a periodic re-emergence. Nor is there a fixed number of social virtues and human wrongs, let alone an overarching consensus on them. As with the idea of the good life, some of the most fundamental disagreements revolve around a more individualist or a more relational conception of human nature: a focus on the individual whose origins we can trace to Descartes, Locke, Hobbes and Kant, or an accentuation of relationality which we can find in Plato, Augustine, Aquinas and Burke.[13]

To recognize that humans are relational and social beings can provide a shared moral horizon for judgements about the virtuous and the wrong. Yet the modern tradition of the social contract from Hobbes and Locke via Rousseau and Kant to John Rawls and Jürgen Habermas posits the sovereign individual who delegates power to the sovereign collective with little mediation between them. What is missing is the idea of covenants that endow social ties with meaning. Burke, for example, emphasizes the irreducible relationality of humans that underpins reciprocal relations. We are born into social relationships: 'the little platoon we belong to in society is the first principle (the germ as it were) of public affections'.[14] These relationships are the first object of our affections. We learn to love and care for family, neighbours and friends. This love creates a sense of attachment and belonging that extends to our fellow citizens and residents as well as to the extended circle of humankind.

Contemporary politics in its liberal, populist or authoritarian guise has little to say about our social nature. We are embodied beings who are embedded in relationships, institutions and the practice of rituals. They command affection and forge attachment as they are rooted in people's identity and interests. These 'public affections', as Burke called them, are indispensable to the good functioning of the rule of law. They build trust and cooperation, which cannot be mandated by rules or regulations. Going beyond social capital and even the exchange of esteem, Burke's emphasis on affective attachment captures something fundamental about our human nature, which Midgley puts well:

> the reality of affectionate bonds among social animals is now fully documented by ethnologists. Their sociability is not just a means to an end. [...] Of course this affection does not mean that they love each other unconditionally. [...] They will in many circumstances compete with and attack each other. But they do all this against a wider background of mutual emotional dependency and friendly acceptance.[15]

Far from being just an appeal to subjective sentiment, Burke's conception of affective attachment shifts the focus to the 'principled practice' of mutual recognition based on human relationality upon which a prosperous market economy and a vibrant democracy depend. Burke's appeal to love and friendship reflects the Aristotelian primacy of relationships over impersonal mechanisms. The practice of lived fraternity can shape a politics of affective attachment to people, place and purpose.

Underpinning this is a certain relation between the individual and the community. The individual will in an asocial, atomized context is arbitrary and without purpose. Individual autonomy and choice, when unmediated by community, or by inherited or shared ethical standards, or by tradition, are meaningless. The meaning of individuality only and always becomes clear within a social context. The community is not some backwards or arbitrary restraint on individual flourishing or self-realization: it is the necessary precondition for it. Individuals only flourish within the content of shared standards, social relationships and the institutions, rituals and practices which sustain them. Individuality without community is empty and community without individuality is oppressive. A postliberal politics seeks to save both by building a balance between them. Achieving this will require a public square that is plural while at the same time upholding the common good against attempts to impose divisive values linked to sectional interests. Postliberalism encourages a political contest which is framed by social virtues to build a new radical centre beyond ideological extremes that serves as a battleground for ideas.

7

Mutual obligations

Nobody saw the summer 2020 protests coming. Yet one prophetic book, Christopher Lasch's 1995 *The Revolt of the Elites and the Betrayal of Democracy*, anatomized our age of elite anger and the underlying culture of narcissism.[1] 'Once it was the "revolt of the masses" that was held to threaten social order and the civilizing traditions of Western culture,' Lasch writes with reference to José Ortega y Gasset's eponymous book.[2] 'In our time, however, the chief threat seems to come from those at the top of the social hierarchy, not the masses.'[3] He could have been writing about the year 2020, which saw the triumph of hyper-capitalism and extreme identity politics: 'the revolt of the elites' against the popular majority with its sense of mutual obligations towards family and fellow citizens, neighbourhoods and nation.

'It is not just that the masses have lost interest in revolution,' he argues: 'their political instincts are demonstrably more conservative than those of their self-appointed spokesmen and would-be liberators.'[4] It is the small-c conservative dispositions of many ordinary people that are not represented by the dominant elites in politics, business or the media. For Lasch, this is a cultural and a class issue, not an ideological one of left

80

versus right: 'It is the working and lower middle classes, after all, who favor limits on abortion, cling to the two-parent family as a source of stability in a turbulent world, resist experiments with "alternative lifestyles," and harbor deep reservations about affirmative action and other ventures in large-scale social engineering.'[5] Since the time of Lasch's writing, social attitudes in the US and UK have on the whole become much more liberal, but if anything the values divide between an increasingly radicalized upper middle class and the rest is growing.

One reason why Lasch's analysis was so prescient is because he critiqued the emerging consensus from within the left, questioning the dogma of progress and the culture of individualism promoted by a 'new class' of professionals and managers who are much more interested in their own social status than in economic justice or political pluralism. This mirrors much of the contemporary far left with its focus on smashing statues and ransacking small shops often owned by working-class immigrants, in alliance with big billion-dollar businesses and the mainstream media, who share the commitment to relentless commodification and the disdain for ordinary people. Lasch puts this well: 'The growing insularity of elites means, among other things, that political ideologies lose touch with the concerns of ordinary citizens.'[6] As a result, the new class has a thin sense of obligation and has 'retained many of the vices of aristocracy without its virtues', lacking the sense of 'reciprocal obligation between the favoured few and the multitude'.[7]

A sense of limits

Far from glorifying aristocratic virtues reserved for the few or the moralism of the self-righteous bourgeoisie,

Lasch argued for a new conception of mutual obligation anchored in common culture and a sense of limits. Our first obligation is to respect natural, human and social limits. Lasch's emphasis on restraint, which echoes Burke's conception of 'that state of things in which liberty is secured by equality of restraint', is key to limiting vice and human wrongs.[8] Here it is worth quoting Burke at some length:

> Men are qualified for civil liberty, in exact proportion to their disposition to put moral chains upon their own appetites; in proportion as their love of justice is above their rapacity; in proportion as their soundness and sobriety of understanding is above their vanity and presumption; in proportion as they are more disposed to listen to the counsels of the wise and good, in preference to the flattery of knaves. Society cannot exist unless a controlling power upon will and appetite be placed somewhere, and the less of it there is within, the more there must be without. It is ordained in the eternal constitution of things, that men of intemperate minds cannot be free. Their passions forge their fetters.[9]

The fundamental difference between ruling elites and ordinary people is not primarily ideological or party political. It is ethical. Elite obsession with separate status or with boundless progress violates a popular sense of shared customs and of intrinsic limits on human power to control society, nature and the body. For Lasch, true social advancement is the sense of obligation that every generation has to improve its inheritance and pass it on to the next – economically, socially and ecologically.

That is why Lasch became increasingly opposed to both the New Left and the New Right. During the Reagan years, he rejected the New Right's economic orthodoxy of wealth disparity masquerading as market competition based on supposedly equal opportunity. Rising inequality is both materially damaging and morally corrupting, as it entails the use of political power for private gain and the erosion of Republican virtue along with the hollowing out of the middle class and the collapse of national cohesion.

Lasch was equally critical of the New Left, holding it responsible for the decline of a common culture under attack from 1960s radicalism and from the progressive movement, which equated its self-serving values with the interests of society as a whole. The writer Ed West summarizes Lasch's thought very well:

> If there were no common values to hold people together, what was to stop the rich and powerful trampling over the rest of society, cloaking their self-interest in furious self-righteousness? And so it has come to pass, with the rise of woke capital, an amoral business model in which CEOs make thousands of times more than their lowest earners, all the while distracting attention with support for therapeutic but increasingly extreme politics. It was Lasch who saw more clearly than anyone that the New Left had a symbiotic relationship with the culture of modern corporate capitalism – emphasising choice, therapy, self-actualisation, narcissism and the rejection of limits, not just physical but financial and moral.[10]

National and international duties

For Lasch, a thick sense of obligation means that wealth carries civic duties. Public libraries, parks, universities, museums, music halls, hospitals, hospices and other civic institutions endowed by old elites stood as monuments to munificence. Of course, there was much selfishness involved in these acts of generous charity (Mandeville's mantra 'private vice, public virtue' comes to mind), besides the fact that a lot of the wealth came from the slave trade and other forms of appalling exploitation. But public generosity – another social virtue – meant that the wealthy participated up to a point in the life of the community and contributed to that of future generations.

Similarly, Lasch's richer conception of obligation means that power implies care for others. Just as property rights are neither absolute nor free from duties, so too political authority requires popular consent and compassion for the most vulnerable. In functioning democracies, power received from the people has to be returned to them by promoting popular agency: their ability to shape their lives and the world around them. That requires personal rule within constitutional checks and balances rather than impersonal forces that can override formal constraints or subvert substantive arrangements. More than a quarter of a century ago, Lasch lamented this evolution:

> Obligation, like everything else, has been deperson-alized; exercised through the agency of the state, the burden of supporting it falls not on the professional and managerial class but, disproportionately, on the lower middle and working classes. The policies advanced by new-class liberals on behalf of the downtrodden and oppressed – racial integration of the public schools, for example – require sacrifices from the ethnic minorities who share the inner cities with the poor, seldom from the suburban liberals who design and support those policies.[11]

The reverse side of the elite culture of narcissism is a culture of indifference to others. Not only the lower classes, for whom elites have contempt. Nor national industry, which they sold off. Nor national public services, which they opt out from. Worse, Lasch also diagnosed elite indifference to their national obligations as a whole: their country, culture and customs. Finance, tech platforms and the dominant political classes are all part of a global moneyed elite more loyal to Davos than to Denver or Dagenham. Today's plutocracy is just the opposite of the old aristocracy's sense of *noblesse oblige* where status comes with duties. Many elites have no substantive conception of democracy and citizenship, which are debased and become merely functional arrangements to advance the interests of a new cosmopolitan class.

For them, the formal mechanisms of democracy are a cipher for popular consent to the rule of power and money, while citizenship offers a passport for free movement. Without a sense of attachment to the nation, the ruling oligarchy lacks any sense of sacrifice or responsibility for their actions. By avoiding tax and exploiting workers, 'they have managed to relieve themselves, to a remarkable extent, of the obligation to contribute to the national treasury. Their acknowledgment of civic obligations does not extend beyond their own immediate neighborhoods.'[12] The future Lasch foresaw is our present: elite enclaves enclosed within a wasteland.

Lasch emphasizes the nexus between the decline of nations and the collapse of the middle class, which is linked to the forces of globalization, capitalism and technology. Like Michael Lind and Christophe Guilluy today, he was right twenty-five years ago to argue that much of the working and lower middle classes have shared interests in improving their lot, anchored in common customs without which the economy and society would dissolve: fair play, contribution, care for loved ones, the dignity of labour and of the person as well as the intrinsic worth of nature.

Here we can go further than Lasch or Lind to suggest that there are mutual obligations beyond nation-states. Common customs connect us to people not only within bounded polities but also across borders. To fellow workers who face exploitation in countries that outlaw or restrict free trade unions. To minorities like the Uighur, who face a state campaign of genocidal persecution. To communities and countries with whom we have historical and cultural ties: in the case of the UK, former foes like France or Germany or former colonies that are an integral part of the Commonwealth. To places of outstanding beauty that are vital for the world's ecological balance, like the Amazon rainforest or the Great Barrier Reef. To sites of universal cultural value, like those on UNESCO's World Heritage list. And much else besides.

A fundamental question arises: are there any specific obligations that we owe to the fellow citizens and residents of our country over and above universal human obligations? In the tradition of virtue ethics, the pursuit of the good life presupposes the community of the polis or city-state, as for Plato and Aristotle. Other ancient thinkers, like the Stoics, envisaged a universal empire or cosmopolis. Today the dominant class of ultraliberals prefers a world of individual atomized exchange underwritten by an ideology of globalism, whereas most authoritarians seek salvation in the creed of nationalism and the sovereign power of the nation-state. Neither commands sustained majority support.

The task for postliberals is to reject these extremes in favour of a radical middle that binds together the local with the national and the global. Postliberalism defends local communities, nations and a national sense of belonging combined with lived solidarity that extends to other nations based on reciprocal obligations to cooperate and assist – in emergencies as well as mutually beneficial opportunities. Such an internationalism involves new modes of cooperation on shared interests for the sake of mutual flourishing: dignified work, security, the building of safe communities and the joint protection of our 'common home of nature', as Pope Francis put it in his 2015 social encyclical *Laudato Si'*.[13] We can learn from the tradition of ethical socialism that grew out of the mutual obligations and lived solidarity among workers and that regarded all human beings as workers in one crucial aspect of their humanity, which is the capacity for creativity and craft.[14]

Renewing democracy and citizenship

Key to the balancing of national with international obligations is a richer conception of democracy and citizenship, which are hollowed out by liberal technocracy and authoritarian coercion alike. Democracy is not only about political rule within a given territory but also a partnership between the generations based on reciprocal duties and anchored in a common inheritance that often, but not always, coincides with national borders. Obligations to others involve loyalty and sympathy with the people around us: family, neighbours, colleagues, fellow citizens and people from elsewhere. The strangers in our midst become our neighbours and part of our communities.[15]

At the same time, not everyone has an equal claim to our affections. We cannot love all humans equally. Equality and respect for dignity extend to the stranger, but they do not abolish the importance of kin, tribe and nation – each constituted by a complex web of interpersonal relationships of reciprocity. Major John

A public philosophy of postliberalism

Cartwright, the early nineteenth-century campaigner for parliamentary reform, put this well: 'Our family, our parish, our country, are the immediate spheres in which, by the limitation of our faculties and the boundedness of our powers, Providence has required us to perform in an especial manner the duties of a Christian.'[16]

Like liberal democracy, liberal citizenship privileges individual rights and entitlements over obligations to others and contribution as a precondition for rewards. This conception is based on the principles of fairness, equality and liberty. The focus on individual rights follows from the assumption that pluralist societies cannot agree on any notion of the common good or even particular goods and that any attempt to define the good would lead to an authoritarian imposition that is contrary to justice. In the work of John Rawls or Ronald Dworkin, justice in terms of ground-rules of fairness gives a status to the poor that is missing from the liberal tradition of Locke to Mill. Toleration of difference and fundamental freedoms are recognized as pillars of a just society.

A richer conception links citizenship to social virtues and starts with the belief that duties beget rights and that privileges have to be earned, as mentioned in the opening chapter. In a radical break with liberal individualism, such an approach shifts the emphasis from sovereign self-interest to making contributions as a way of earning entitlements. Contribution defines the body politic with its duties and rights. Of course, making contributions is not limited to paid employment but encompasses all manner of unpaid jobs, still mostly done by women, which require much greater public recognition, economic reward and social status.

Virtuous citizenship elevates people from the virtual world of atomized exchange to the real place of relationships, institutions, agency, statecraft and leadership. Linked to duty and obligation are vocation and service: nurturing our particular and even unique talents to serve others in the community and the country. The importance of more virtue alongside greater popular participation in power is clear when we consider the sharp decline of trust in leading institutions: Parliament, parties, judges, the churches and mainstream media like the BBC. Despite the virtues of individual members, these organizations are characterized by an inverse relationship between a lack of transparency and accountability and an excess of moral corruption and unchecked elitism.

Recognizing reciprocity

Honouring mutual obligations will require the greater presence of social virtues in the public realm, combined with renewed covenantal ties between the state at all levels and its dispersed citizens. Postliberalism begins with the recognition that most people's greatest concern is for their loved ones: their obligations to parents and children, wider family and friends. Another concern is with the places people inhabit and how to make them safe, prosperous and beautiful. A stronger, more devolved democracy based on redistributing power coupled with resources is as vital as a renewal of virtue capable of educating everyone into citizenship with its duties and rights. In short, postliberalism is organized around the everyday experience of family, friends and place, of work, wages and public goods – of all the complex relationships and institutions that make life worth living.

Published posthumously in 1995 after Lasch's death from cancer the previous year, *Revolt of the Elites* foretold the deepening divisions in the US brought about by 1960s political radicalism and 1980s free-market fundamentalism, which have now reached new levels of socio-economic cataclysm. Indeed, Lasch anticipated the left's economically liberal turn in the 1990s and the ultraliberal fusion of market fundamentalism with identity politics in the 2010s. As he wrote, 'The revolt of the masses that Ortega feared is no longer a plausible threat. But the revolt of the elites against time-honored traditions of locality, obligation, and restraint may yet unleash a war of all against all.'[17] Where does this leave postliberalism? As the Hobbesian bellum *omnium contra omnes* now unfolds, a postliberal politics has to combine scepticism with hopefulness: a healthy sceptical attitude towards all utopian projects with their dystopian consequences, while being hopeful that realistic, viable alternatives anchored in the nurturing of social virtue and mutual obligations might emerge. It is what we owe ourselves and generations past, present and future.

8

Pluralism

In a remarkable essay written two years after New Labour came to power in 1997, the British academic and former Labour MP David Marquand criticized what he called the centralizing, populist instincts of Tony Blair's government, which ignored the decentralizing, pluralist checks and balances of Britain's mixed constitution. Commenting on Blair's wide-ranging constitutional reforms (including the Human Rights Act and the three devolved administrations), Marquand qualified it as 'a revolution without a theory. It is the muddled, messy work of practical men and women, unintellectual when not positively anti-intellectual, apparently oblivious of the long tradition of political and constitutional reflection of which they are the heirs.'[1] On a different scale and intensity, this applies to the Johnson government with its prorogation of Parliament (contrary to the principles of parliamentary sovereignty and parliamentary scrutiny of the executive), attacks on the civil service and breaches of international law 'in a limited and specific way'. It is an interesting reflection on the dangers of top-down anti-elite populism by a new class. In keeping with the spirit of Christopher Lasch, we could call it 'rulers' revolt' (though in Johnson's case, it is of course true that the Remainer establishment tried to thwart Brexit every step of the way).

Elite anti-pluralism

The tradition Marquand invokes rests on the pluralism of parliamentary sovereignty with Crown-in-Parliament and the intertwining of the executive, legislature and judiciary. This imperfect and unstable balance was fatally undermined when Blair removed the Law Lords from the upper chamber and created a US-inspired Supreme Court. Devolution, though the intention was in part honourable, created a lopsided structure that allowed nationalist forces in Scotland and increasingly also in Wales to become dominant while leaving England as a nation unrepresented within the Union. Far from rebalancing the disparities of wealth and power across Britain, the pattern of overcentralized power combined with weak ineffective institutions was transferred from London to Edinburgh and Cardiff. Something similar has happened with city-regions and is likely to occur with the 'levelling up' agenda: delegation of responsibilities without devolving power or resources. The effect of populism – whether Blair's elite ultraliberal variant or Johnson's insurgent antiliberal version – is to make the polity even less plural.

As Marquand points out,

> Pluralism is not a doctrine. It is a disposition, a mentality, an approach. Like most approaches to politics, it is a matter of feeling as well as of belief. Pluralists rejoice in variety. They are sceptical about theories – Marxism, economic liberalism, globalisation – that presuppose uniformity. Pluralists like the clash and clang of argument; the monochrome sameness of the big

battalions horrifies them; so does the sugary conformism of the politically correct. Instinctively, they are for the 'little platoons' that Edmund Burke saw as the nurseries of 'public affections', and they want to protect them from the homogenising pressures of state, market and opinion. For them, a good society is a mosaic of vibrant smaller collectivities – trade unions, universities, business associations, local authorities, miners' welfares, churches, mosques, Women's Institutes, NGOs – each with its own identity, tradition, values and rituals.[2]

Besides democracy and citizenship, postliberalism has to renew such a conception of political pluralism against both liberal and authoritarian monism: the attempt to iron out plurality by an oligarchy that concentrates power and wealth. As already mentioned, this parallelism in no way implies moral equivalence. Liberalism seeks to uphold liberty and equality, and certain liberal traditions do preserve fundamental freedoms. Regardless of liberal excesses, authoritarianism is politically and ethically far more dangerous. It tends to subsume the liberty of each and the equality of all under the sovereign power of a self-serving collective leadership. Authoritarian systems extend state surveillance into all spheres of societal and personal life, co-opting any independent movement and persecuting non-conformist groups.

One of the worst contemporary examples is the treatment of the Uighurs in China's north-western region of Xinjiang, who have suffered imprisonment in 're-education' camps and forced sterilization. After Uighur militants killed thirty-one Han Chinese in 2014, China's Communist Party leader Xi Jinping ordered local officials to respond 'with absolutely no mercy [...] the weapons of the people's democratic dictatorship should be wielded without any hesitation or wavering'.[3]

The aim is both brainwashing the existing population and over time wiping out the Uighur people altogether. As the Xinjiang papers published by *The New York Times* revealed, the family members of those imprisoned in the re-education camps were told that 'their thinking has become infected with unhealthy thoughts. Freedom is only possible when the virus in their thinking is eradicated.'[4] In the Uighur regions of Kashgar and Hotan, the number of births collapsed by over 60 per cent in the years 2015–18, while Beijing now pushes pro-natalist policies for Han Chinese. This genocidal campaign is a particularly gruesome example of authoritarian anti-pluralism with totalitarian tendencies.

Liberal-authoritarian monism

Beyond these fundamental differences, certain liberal and authoritarian systems leave societies homogenized and atomized both at once: concentrating wealth and power in the hands of new classes while destroying most autonomous and democratically self-governing intermediary institutions. Ultraprogressives take the liberal principle of individual autonomy so far as to override all barriers to free choice, while identitarians reject liberal individualism and shut down public debate by enforcing an intolerant creed of 'cancel culture' that erodes plural voices (as discussed in Chapter 3). For their part, authoritarians pay lip service to social conservatism whereas in reality they import capitalist commodification that erodes social and cultural pluralism. Some liberals in the ultraprogressivist vein imagine they can deconstruct the non-liberal, authoritarian traits of culture – family, taboos on drugs or religion – but what they really deconstruct are the works of liberalism itself, including the social contract that rests on notions of solidarity and fair play.

Similarly, authoritarians suppose they can protect their societies from the corrupting tendencies of liberalism – moral relativism, weak states – but what they really do is to undermine the social basis of their political authority. For example, opening up their countries to the liberal forces of capitalism, technology and globalization undermines the cultural norms on which their claim to legitimacy rests. Neither liberalism nor authoritarianism can secure the political or cultural pluralism that is key to vibrant economies and healthy societies.

Different strands of liberalism purport to be pluralist yet end up being monist. One such strand is the agonistic liberalism of Isaiah Berlin and Joseph Raz, which claims that any invocation of the good goes against incommensurable values. Since there can be no valid agreement about standards of goodness or any other substantive consent among individuals, the only available basis for peaceful coexistence is the respect for the sacrosanct principle of negative liberty: absence of constraints on free choice except the law and private conscience.[5] Another strand is the already-mentioned liberal legalism of John Rawls and Richard Dworkin, who emphasize the positivity of individual rights in place of the metaphysical good. Because the latter will always be a source of conflict and violence, we can only agree to disagree and put in place some basic ground rules of fairness, for anything else would violate negative freedom and the 'overlapping consensus'.[6]

In each case, a sham appeal to pluralism is used to silence critics and enforce a single ideology. It is precisely negative freedom, the 'overlapping consensus' and utility maximization that are the enemies of pluralism and tolerance, because they impose a single, homogeneous and uniform set of standards on everybody: mutually self-interested contract instead of real mutual agreement; an often assumed collective volition to the detriment of free association; and aggregate utility instead of the diverse but coordinated flourishing of both persons and groups. The *more* that liberal pluralism posits nothing but a clash of incommensurable values, then the *more also* a purely rational and utilitarian logic must govern the public process of mitigating inevitable anarchic diversity. Hence the appeal to exclusively negative freedom, individual rights and subjective happiness, for none of them involve any substantive negotiation or conciliation around shared interests.

As the central state and the global market concentrate ever more power linked to wealth, the spaces in which people can negotiate to reconcile estranged interests continue to shrink. Local government has been decimated. Trade unions have been curtailed or lost their relevance. Workplace democracy in the UK or the US was never properly built. And communities lack resources to act on behalf of their members. A programme of institution building and policy reform has to be grounded in the sources of political pluralism: a complex mixed constitution, multiple corporate bodies and the dignity of the person.

Building a pluralist polity

A pluralist constitution favours a complex body politic based on the freedom of association, which means that people can freely associate around certain shared ends: education, housing, health, but also political or other causes, as with registered charities that protect a country's cultural inheritance or places of outstanding natural beauty. Associations rest on the reality that humans are social, political beings who together pursue common goals, even if they are always contested and life in society always involves both cooperation and conflict. Building a common life also involves more than contracts or the law. The interaction of rights and obligations involved in contractual relations requires more than legal-contractual ties because trust and cooperation cannot be mandated by law or enforced through coercive means.

Free and democratically self-governing associations are about collective action serving mutually beneficial interests. This is neither the global marketplace of individual atomized exchange promoted by the dominant strands of liberalism nor state centralism reducing people to administrative units as favoured by authoritarian systems. Plural spaces in which political decisions are made with greater popular participation require a variety of associations. They give rise to corporate bodies and intermediary institutions through which persons or groups can exercise political agency. The late Paul Hirst's work on associative democracy and the political tradition on which it draws (John Neville Figgis and G.D.H. Cole) provide as yet unrealized resources to renew the body politic.[7]

Constitutionally guaranteed freedom of association is key in pluralizing the state and balancing the three branches of government, so that neither dominates the others. When this is lacking, the political process is paralysed – as is the case in the US and increasingly in the UK, where either executive writ rides roughshod over Parliament (from Thatcher to Blair and from Cameron to Johnson) or parliamentary proceduralism combined with Whitehall bureaucracy stops bold reform.

A public philosophy of postliberalism

Constitutionalist conceptions of the polity differ fundamentally from contractualist theories of the state, which view persons or groups in formal terms as individual or collective units. The Italian legal historian Paolo Grossi describes contractualism as positing 'the unitary subject of natural law, an a-historical and therefore merely virtual subject, a model of man and no more'. By contrast, constitutionalism is about 'an intrinsically *relational* entity, well-entrenched in a cultural, social and economic context, found alongside another, all others, and having a very close and necessary relationship with them'.[8]

Besides the importance of autonomous bodies within the body politic, a constitutionalist conception accentuates the human disposition towards mutual recognition rather than the mere pursuit of political power or economic wealth. Mutual recognition implies that humans are relational beings, embedded in relationships and institutions that enable them to organize life in society in which the economy and politics are ensconced.[9] Free and democratically self-governing associations build on the idea that human beings are at heart relational – rather than isolated individuals or subsumed under a single collective. Humanity is a complex compact of relational beings bound together by a common outlook: a natural desire for mutual flourishing, shared prosperity and the public good based on shared interests. The following passage from the eighteenth-century thinker Antonio Genovesi, who was a near contemporary of Adam Smith's and held one of the first chairs in political economy, expresses this particularly well:

> Every person has a natural and intrinsic obligation to study how to procure his happiness; but the political body is made of persons; therefore the entire political

body and each of its members is obligated to do his part, i.e. all that he knows and can do for common prosperity, as long as that which is done does not offend the rights of the other civil bodies. This obligation, from the civil body, with beautiful and divine ties, returns to each family and each person for the common pacts of the society. Each family and every person are under two obligations to do that which they can to procure public happiness: one comes from within nature, and the other comes from the subsequent pacts of communities. A third obligation can be added, that of one's own utility. That which Shaftesbury said will be eternally true: he said that the true utility is the daughter of virtue; because it is eternally true that the great depth of man is the love for those with whom he lives. This is the love that is the daughter of virtue.[10]

Renewing corporatism

The second source of political pluralism are autonomous corporate bodies that constitute society. This is emphatically not the same as the state corporatism of 1930s and 1940s totalitarian systems, which absorbed all intermediary institutions into the central state at the service of coercion and total war. As Lenin infamously said, in communism trade unions are 'transmission belts between the party and the people'. The same applied to fascism and national socialism. In constitutionally plural systems, by contrast, intermediary institutions are independent of both the central state and the free market. Democratic corporatism is about the sharing of power and wealth across society. Corporate bodies that are democratically governed, including professional associations, universities and local community organizations, play a key role in giving people a voice and collective action in a world dominated by the impersonal forces of the central state and the global economy.

Unmediated state sovereignty on the model of Machiavelli's Prince or Hobbes' Leviathan risks authoritarian control at home and anarchy abroad. Only autonomous, intermediary institutions can uphold a plural democracy. As if he was anticipating a pandemic, Marquand wrote in the above-mentioned essay, 'Thomas Hobbes, the philosopher of absolute sovereignty, famously compared such collectivities to "worms in the entrails of a natural man". Pluralists see them as antibodies protecting the culture of democracy from infection.'[11] Only by renewing the institutions and relationships of civic society will countries become resilient to the pandemics of the future. The response to the viral emergency has already seen a new impetus to corporatist bargaining between the state, business, trade unions and the charitable sector. Across much of the West, we are witnessing how the voluntary involvement of civic groups is essential for the sustaining of agriculture, education, welfare and people's mental and physical health. But so far the new corporatism depends too much on the will of the executive and on central resources.

Rather than being ruled by state power, a corporatist polity is meant to constrain it within a balanced institutional ecology. New trade unions in the gig economy are just as vital as decentralized democracy and laws to regulate or break up corporate monopolies, beginning with the big banks and the tech platforms. Otherwise US libertarian free-marketeers or Chinese state capitalists will take over weakened businesses. A more interventionist state alone will not be able to resist this. If a plural and democratic corporatism between estranged interests can be negotiated, then confederal cooperation across borders is equally possible. And if relationships and institutions trump individualism, then the nation-state is surely part of a nested network of peoples and nations and not absolutely sovereign because it is but the individual writ large. Democratic nations need to nurture together an international settlement of what Michael Lind calls 'wards in the realm of government, guilds in the realm of the economy and congregations in the realm of culture'[12] – each being membership institutions with countervailing power on behalf of citizens against vested interests.

The promise of personalism

The third source of political pluralism is personalism, which rejects the secular logic of modern binaries – especially left versus right and individual versus collective – in favour of the idea that we live in webs of relationships, formed through imitative action, yet such that the relational bond permitting imitation is always already there, as with parenthood, friendship, local community and the workplace. Personalist thinkers, such as Emmanuel Mounier, Henri de Lubac, Luigi Sturzo or Max Scheler, also made the paradoxical but coherent connection between individual uniqueness and relationality. Whereas the isolated liberal individual increasingly becomes a bare atom (ironically replaceable by any other atom), the embedded person enjoys both a unique perspective and unique attributes. Such a real, 'rounded' person possesses worth that exceeds the price of commodities or the value of administrative units.

Mounier, thinking in the traditions of 'French spiritualism' stretching back to Maine de Biran in the late eighteenth and early nineteenth century, locates the very heart of personalism in the circumstance that humans have a unique power to transform their environment, yet are forever faced with the problems which this presents them with.[13] These problems include 'alienation' for the Hegelian-Marxist tradition and the formation of relatively good or bad habits for the Biranian one. To be a person is to become ever more personal by trying to perfect relations and seeking the goods internal to human activity: being a good parent, worker, spouse, athlete, neighbour and citizen.

Negotiating these problems always involves for Mounier an accentuation of three sites of mediation: the body (here echoing the phenomenologist Maurice Merleau-Ponty), property and the family. In the excesses of either Marxism or liberalism, these are all to be regarded as non-owned 'openings' to all the vagaries of both nature and culture. Their givenness mediates what lies beyond their reach: the space of souls where, as St Augustine stressed, we can all enjoy non-competitively something good without rivalry, like sunlight (foreshadowed by Plato in the allegory of the cave). The seventeenth-century English poet Thomas Traherne puts this beautifully:

> I was guided by an implicit faith in God's goodness: and therefore led to the study of the most obvious and common things. For thus I thought within myself: God being, as we generally believe, infinite in goodness, it is most consonant and agreeable with His nature, that the best things should be most common. For nothing is more natural to infinite goodness, than to make the best things most frequent; and only things worthless scarce. Then I began to enquire what things were most common: Air, Light, Heaven and Earth, Water, the Sun, Trees, Men and Women, Cities, Temples, &c. These I found common and obvious to all: Rubies, Pearls,

Diamonds, Gold and Silver; these I found scarce, and to the most denied. Then began I to consider and compare the value of them which I measured by their serviceableness, and by the excellencies which would be found in them, should they be taken away. And in conclusion, I saw clearly, that there was a real valuableness in all the common things; in the scarce, a feigned.[14]

The public goods that can be shared simultaneously and non-exclusively stretch from more 'material' ones, like air or oceans, to more immaterial ones, like friendship or community. In between there are many more relational goods – including health, education, trust and cooperation – which are linked to social interaction.[15] Groups, not the isolated individual or the anonymous collective, are key to producing and consuming such goods, and it is in groups that individuals become more rounded persons just because they cannot by themselves alone bring about the shared reality.

In addition, personalism insists on the irreducibility of soul to body, with mind or spirit comprising both, as for the monotheistic faiths and strands within other world religions as well as certain humanist traditions. The historical origins of this conception of the 'integral' human person can be traced to the so-called Axial Age (800–200 BC), when the great philosophies of East and West emerged together with faith traditions. In Plato, Buddha, Confucius, the Old Testament prophets and later Jesus, they converged around two arguments: first, a rejection of absolutist power underwritten by gods who were not believed to be on the side of ordinary humans; and, second, the belief that personal flourishing is connected with a transcendent outlook that refuses sacrificial practices to appease divine wrath and instead favours the dignity of the person.[16]

A public philosophy of postliberalism

In short, pluralism in the most liberal – that is, generous – sense breaks down the artificial divide between individual and collective, left and right, state and market, as well as immanence and transcendence. It is properly paradoxical, which Maurice Glasman defines as 'something that sounds wrong but is right [...] such as tradition shapes modernity, faith will redeem citizenship, trust is the basis of competition, contribution strengthens solidarity, labour power improves competitiveness, decentralisation underpins patriotism'.[17] Central to this is the personal origin of human society and work as the free expression of unique personhood. The dignity of labour means that all jobs should have worth and all workers status – including non-paid work mostly performed by women. Faced with the impersonal mechanisms of the bureaucratic state and the global market, this perspective puts the person back at the centre. A personalist politics populates notions of dignity and the common good with tangible meaning: reward for contribution based on caring, earning and belonging.

Politics as practical wisdom

To say all this is to defend human free will and our powers of discernment and judgement, without which democracy in the best sense of people sharing in the exercise of sovereign power would lose all ground of possibility. This brings us back to Aristotle's practical wisdom or *phronêsis*, which should be at the heart of politics: an ethical art or moral tact that links human intention to virtuous skill. Without such an integrated conception, social judgement will be stripped from the hands of humans as workers who are *homo faber*

104

– creative beings – and desire relationality, creative fulfilment in work, festivity and joy.

For Aristotle, the aim of politics is to nurture flourishing citizens, which means instilling virtuous practices in social and economic relations and fostering the formation of character. The aim of social and economic relations will not be mainly the satisfaction of private preferences but the service of the public good with all its particular relational goods. The widest possible personalist framework is the *polis* with its mixed constitution. Yet relationships and institutions cross the boundaries of states. Therefore, the broadest scope of just reciprocal exchange of relational goods between persons is the international society of cities, regions, nations and cultural commonwealths – socially and culturally shared ties between peoples. Pluralism tries to hold patriotism in balance with internationalism.

Where does that leave democracy or citizenship? In his above-cited essay, Marquand does not offer an answer to this question. But he makes the point that populism is aligned with individualism because both rest on the erosion of intermediary institutions and a lack of character and dispersed leadership. To foster a pluralist politics, countries require a democratic system based on robust debate and educative guidance:

> Ours is a populist age – demotic, sentimental, resentful of excellence. To be sure, it is also a hyper-individualistic age. But despite appearances to the contrary, populism and hyper-individualism go together. A mass of disaggregated individuals, in a society where intermediate institutions have been hollowed out, is more likely to respond to a populist appeal than to any other. Populist languages make no demands on their listeners. They flatter the emotions; they promise the isolated and

alienated membership of a greater whole; above all, they place the burdens of freedom on the leader's shoulders.

In the last resort, however, the case against the populist mentality is moral, not practical. It has to do with the nature of democracy. The populist argument for democracy is that the people should be sovereign. Accept that, and populism prevails. But it is not the only argument – or the best. The pluralist vision of democracy implies a deliberative, reflective politics of power-sharing and mutual education. Absolute popular sovereignty is as alien to it as absolute parliamentary sovereignty.[18]

Building a plural politics is never complete. It is the work of centuries. But each generation has a duty to try, and the post-Covid world offers us a glimmer of possibility.

9

Place, limits and ecology

The coronavirus crisis seems to have started at the Huanan seafood market in the city of Wuhan, where the viral stowaways of bats spilled over into humans. Epidemiological experts call this a 'super-spreading event'. Cheap flights abroad increased this super-spreading event exponentially, allowing a local plague to become a global pandemic. But the conditions for viral spill-over go much further than mass tourism, animal cruelty or a lack of hygiene in Chinese 'wet markets'. Land use and climate change are fundamental factors. A combination of habitat destruction, intensive agriculture and humanly induced global warming has forced animals into ever-smaller habitats in close proximity to urban settlements. According to a recent report by the conservation group World Wildlife Fund, wildlife populations have declined by more than two-thirds in less than fifty years. This catastrophic collapse shows no signs of slowing down as humans destroy wild areas, over-fish the seas and burn forests.[1] The relentless expansion by humans into previously wild habitats dramatically diminishes the world's wildlife into confined spaces, and viruses come bursting out. The viral emergency is a side-effect of the wider climate emergency. Both raise the fundamental question of humanity's place in the natural order and limits on human power so as to try to restore a measure of the world's ecological balance.

Our common home of nature

Both liberals and authoritarians tend to oppose humanity to a single natural order, which they seek either to dominate (as for neoliberalism and authoritarianism) or to liberate from human domination (as for liberal progressives, including much of the Green movement). By contrast, a postliberal public philosophy seeks to think the relationship between the human and the natural by acknowledging our animality but also our freedom, creativity and social nature, which set us apart from other members of the animal kingdom. Beyond laws of nature, postliberalism also acknowledges that the natural world is profoundly complex, spontaneous and unpredictable, which rules out any notion of a fixed nature which we are at liberty to exploit or to which we must surrender.[2] Nor can we calculate a perfect equilibrium where human needs somehow coincide with the supply of natural resources and ecological sustainability – whether through the invisible hand of the market or the clunking fist of the state.

Underwritten by the state, the dominant forces of capitalism and techno-science today are allied against human flourishing within 'our common home of nature'.[3] Like politics and indeed all spheres of human activity, our relationship with the natural world is not reducible to human will but instead requires careful judgement and prudence. We need to be wary of claims

108

about measureless acquisition and endless economic expansion in a finite world in which humankind transgresses all manner of physical and moral boundaries at its own peril. Missing from purely secular thought that denies any possibility of a transcendent outlook on reality is a sense of limits based on self-restraint – limits on our insatiable desires that are artificially produced by a capitalist system combined with what the Anglican socialist R.H. Tawney describes as the acquisitive society.[4]

And as the former Archbishop of Canterbury Rowan Williams suggests in his reading of Pope Francis's *Laudato Si'*, the materialism that characterizes the dominant modern ideologies is in fact deeply anti-material and destructive of nature:

> The plain thereness of the physical world we inhabit tells us from our first emergence into consciousness that our will is not the foundation of everything – and so its proper working is essentially about creative adjustment to an agenda set not by our fantasy but by the qualities and complexities of what we encounter. The material world tells us that to be human is to be in dialogue with what is other: what is physically other, what is humanly other in the solid three-dimensionality of other persons, ultimately what is divinely other.[5]

For Pope Francis, as for Williams, the fundamental issue is the loss of meaning – the intrinsic worth and purpose of human beings, other animals and the entire biosphere. Connected with this is a new culture of 'disposability' in which everyone and everything that does not satisfy our immediate desires can so readily be dispensed with precisely because it has already been turned into a commodity.

Place as the soil of humanity

Against the impersonal and dehumanizing logic of both liberal and authoritarian systems, postliberalism defends the whole person embedded in a wider natural and social order – even if that order is always unstable, and no more so than in post-pandemic times. Unless and until bio-technology or Artificial Intelligence redefines our humanity altogether, nature and society will continue to be more primary than politics or the economy because life transcends the nature/culture divide by fusing material reality with symbolic significance. As contemporary anthropology in the wake of Karl Polanyi's and Marcel Mauss' pioneering work on gift exchange suggests, humans are bound together through practices of mutual recognition, which is mediated by things at once tangible and ineffable.[6] This is how meaning emerges, in both concrete and abstract ways that remain embedded in everyday existence. To remove all location or place from people is to destroy the very soil of their humanity, as Simone Weil argues.[7]

The postliberal accentuation of limit and place is by no means a prelude for a politics of de-growth, as certain strands within radical ecologism advocate. Rather, postliberalism argues for a different kind of economy and material growth. The theologian John Milbank puts this well:

> Ecology is also *not* committed to the idea that the resources of the planet are naturally finite without our intervention: to the contrary, just because they are temporal and self-renewing they are serially infinite. [...] scarcity is something *humanly produced* in order to stimulate competitive demand and increased profit and to tighten centralised control.[8]

110

It is true that resources are scarce in the short term and that their deeply unequal distribution is one of the main proximate causes for human suffering. Over the medium and long run, however, the natural world – combined with human labour, ingenuity and technological innovation – can generate an almost infinite flow of finite resources. With a much more just distribution, the wealth of nature is able to meet humanity's real needs and provide universal basic goods such as food, energy, shelter, healthcare, education, art and friendship.

Besides the key question of how to inject justice into the global distribution of resources, the other principal task is to bring about a fundamental cultural change. How do late modern, capitalist societies find a better balance between, on the one hand, the natural desire for individual autonomy, which is vital for a creative and dignified life, and, on the other hand, the equally natural desire for social relations that limit personal freedom and through self-restraint enable us to build a common life? Limits on consumption and sheer waste are not only ecological imperatives as the destruction of our entire biosphere proceeds apace. They are also economic and ethical imperatives: the need to build up more locally embedded supply lines, which help to reduce dependence on foreign powers we cannot trust and to strengthen regional and national resilience.

Key to such a cultural change is cooperation between different social classes based on shared interests. Liberals have privileged mass mobility and abstraction from place, whereas authoritarians champion national isolation and even atavistic ethno-centrism. Neither speaks to the needs and interests of a popular majority. The space is wide open for a postliberal cross-class coalition bringing together large sections of working- and middle-class people who share a commitment to place. More than twenty-five years ago, Lasch made the point that the middle class are the main agents for a politics of place:

> But the unattractive features of middle-class nationalism [*sic*] should not obscure its positive contributions in the form of a highly developed *sense of place* and a respect for historical continuity – hallmarks of the middle-class sensibility that can be appreciated more fully now that middle-class culture is everywhere in retreat. Whatever its faults, middle-class nationalism provided a common ground, common standards, a common frame of reference without which society dissolves into nothing more than contending factions.[9]

A good example of what Lasch referred to was the re-moralized culture of the Victorian era with extensive pride in local civic institutions, building of libraries, town halls and art galleries – all underpinned by a spirit of solidarity and mutual aid.[10]

Politics of place

With both the middle and working class facing economic and cultural insecurity, recognizing the importance of place is key to a majority politics. Building on Lasch, Christophe Guilluy and Michael Lind are right to highlight the growing gulf between elite enclaves and peripheral wasteland or hub versus heartland. Yet such and similar binaries underplay the disparities of power, wealth and status running through every community. The borough of Kensington at the heart of metropolitan London is home to a royal palace and plenty of foreign billionaires. Within a two-mile radius, there is Grenfell Tower. Its residents are no less excluded from the wealth of the nation than the ex-industrial working class in the provincial heartlands – from Wrexham to Workington, Blythe Valley to Bury, Derby to Darlington, Bolsover to Bishop Auckland, and Scunthorpe to Sedgefield. The task for postliberals is to build a new political coalition across communities, classes and generations so as to be a national force that is embedded in localities.

Since place matters to people everywhere except perhaps the top 2 per cent who are globally mobile, it is vital to reaffirm the centrality of location. The political geographer John Tomaney has shown that 'the local, its cultures and its solidarities are a moral starting point and a locus of ecological concern in all human societies and at all moments of history'.[11] Belonging to a particular place is the starting point, but a strong sense of local identity is compatible with a shared sense of national identity. Land with its material reality and its symbolic significance is central to people's sense of belonging. Beginning with local and national roots does not rule out the possibility of building relationships with people across borders as boundaries are porous – often the result of historically contingent events and politically artificial decisions.

Even the forces of globalization have not eliminated the relevance of geography altogether. Just the opposite: as the author Robert Kaplan reminds us, we forget geography at our own peril.[12] In suggesting that the mapping of mountains, rivers and plains determines destiny, he argues against any economic, technological or demographic determinism and in favour of our spatial condition. We are born into specific places and at the same time find ourselves in a complex web of international connections. As Tomaney points out, 'local identities may provide the conditions for a "progressive" mode of dwelling within these wider processes'.[13] Learning how to inhabit a place is a

A public philosophy of postliberalism

key part of our education into citizenship with the balancing of rights with obligations and the conciliation of interests. Without a sense of place there can be no bounded polity and therefore no democracy. 'Local communities and institutions are social achievements created collectively in face of conflict,' writes Tomaney, 'and roots in "traditional culture" and "community" may provide a basis for collective resistance to inequitable social change.'[14]

A politics of place has to recognize just how important the land is to people's affection for their locality and their attachment to their country. It is an integral part of people's sense of belonging. Nature and the countryside are sources of beauty and well-being as well as economic resources. Yet capitalism and globalization are destroying the delicate equilibria of the ecosystem. Instead of an abstract Green Deal that focuses on the aggregate economy, what is required is an ecological politics that is embedded in local community and speaks to people's concrete existence – an environmentalism attuned to both urban and rural communities, food production and distribution, the welfare of animals and renewal energy supply.

All these concerns involve courage, political imagination and human judgement. They bring us back to the sense of politics as art. It is a recurrent idea in the work of Mary Midgley, whom Roger Scruton praised as follows: 'Believing that philosophy has been wrongly described as the handmaiden of the sciences, she seeks instead to approximate it to art, poetry and religion, as part of a systematic attempt to make sense of the human condition and to show the place in the natural world of beings like us.'[15] Place in its political, cultural and ecological senses is a key theme in postliberalism.

To conclude this part of the book: a postliberal public philosophy is about renewing politics, injecting ideas and reorienting political debate away from a slavish dependence on natural or social science and towards the nurturing of mutual flourishing. Social virtues such as honour, loyalty, duty and practical wisdom are vital for meaningful morality in public life as they help to minimize vice and limit human wrongs. In turn, this will only be possible by placing issues of duty and reciprocal obligations at the core of public discussion. Neither individual and collective will nor atomized exchange can be the basis for rethinking politics. History and memory, not rationalism or economistic science, provide rich sources of renewal. The twin forces of hyper-capitalism and extreme identity politics are eroding those foundations, but so far 'cancel culture' has not abolished reality or redefined human nature altogether. We can articulate a public political philosophy that reflects our natural dispositions towards a plural quest for the public good and flourishing, anchored in a sense of belonging to particular places and people.

III

POLITICAL AND POLICY PROGRAMME

In politics, as Maurice Glasman is fond of reminding us, the entertainer Max Bygraves is a better guide than the philosopher René Descartes. 'Let me tell you a story' is a more promising path to political power than policy prescriptions based on purely rational categories. Yet at the same time, policy is the spear of politics with which we pierce a problem and help bring about transformative change. The final part of the book will therefore outline both a wider narrative and specific policy ideas. But in a short book with a broad scope, new policies cannot be developed in great depth or detail. Much more work will be needed to turn them into concrete policies – though the main obstacle will likely be political, not technical. That is why the book will conclude with some reflections on how to build new coalitions that can change the consensus and put into practice a postliberal politics.

The political and policy programme seeks to build more mutualist markets embedded in the everyday economy, decentralized states, a pluralist democracy, a balance of open economies with protection of domestic industry and a novel corporatism that reconciles the estranged interests of government, capital and labour

117

– based on the dignity of the person reflected in both rights and obligations. Faced with the extremes of globalism and nationalism, the postliberal alternative promotes a new civic internationalism of peoples and nations around democratic association that enables workers to resist the dehumanizing exploitation of contemporary capitalism.

A plural state and mutualist markets require good practice, leadership and new forms of collective agency. Greater social stability and greater regard for our natural environment need a stronger sense of duty, compassion and service. All this needs to be distilled into national stories of renewal anchored in courage and the imagination. That would help Western and other countries engage with the pressing problems of today: the sense of exclusion and estrangement that many people suffer alongside the humiliation and dispossession they experience from the loss of national pride, employment or community; a lack of participation in power and prosperity; the decline of virtue in both private organizations and public institutions. How can politics and policy develop more compassion in the health service, more wisdom in the education system, more relational prosperity in our private sector and more civility across our politics and public realm?

10

Building a relational economy

The worldwide Covid-19 emergency suspended the operation of capitalism for some time but did not transform its fundamental logic. Across the West, the dominant response was to replace a Hayekian/ Friedmanite free-market fundamentalism with neo-Keynesian state activism as governments underwrote the wages of workers and provided emergency loans to distressed businesses. After forty years of near-permanent Thatcherite economics with its focus on maximizing individual choice, this was no trivial change. As the coronavirus crisis accelerates the fragmentation of globalization, the resurgence of the sovereign state could lead to the re-localization of supply chains, the reinvention of industrial policy aimed at greater national self-sufficiency in critical supplies and a new political consensus on greater investment in public services – most notably health and social care. Beyond right- and left-liberal economics, we are witnessing a new age of state intervention in the economy.

Political and policy programme

Two faces of state intervention

The state can be a valuable partner in disrupting the rule of corporate surveillance capitalism and help to create a space in which civic institutions flourish. Government can do good by encouraging and rewarding more virtuous behaviour of both individuals and firms. Yet increased government intervention alone does little more than paper over the cracks of an economic model that leaves most people dispossessed, demoralized and vulnerable. While the strengthening of national government is necessary, absolute state sovereignty favours market expansion into all areas of society, as in the US, or leads to some form of totalitarian state capitalism, as in China. Either way, the sovereign state is more often than not complicit with the exploitation of workers and the commodification of life. Alongside capitalism and mass media (turbocharged by social media), the nation-state – without strong civic institutions and international cooperation – ends up undermining social bonds. As Karl Polanyi argued in his seminal book *The Great Transformation* (1944), the state disembedded from the ties of society subordinates the social to the joint rule of the economic and the political.

Market and state combine to erode the mutual self-organization of people. The tragedy of the post-war settlement was that the complex web of reciprocal obligations between citizens, generations and communities within nations was absorbed by central state power.[1] The more rounded person morphed into the increasingly entitled individual as top-down paternalism replaced communal reciprocity. With the rise of Benthamite utilitarian technocracy and Rawlsian liberal

120

legalism, the conception of citizens as ethical actors with obligations towards others was gradually abandoned in favour of the new notion of mere consumers in pursuit of their own individual happiness.

Compared with the post-war era, power and capital are nowadays far more centralized and concentrated while personal savings have given way to personal debts. The increase in state power has accrued to the benefit of big banking and business. Money redistributed to the peripheries drifts back to the centre as people flock to the booming metropolis. Meanwhile financial aid to the disadvantaged in the broken towns turns into further dependency. For now, the dominant response to Covid-19 reinforces the rule of the nation-state and of capitalism, which together weaken what the historian E.P. Thompson called the 'moral economy' built on 'customs in common'.[2]

Developing the national economy

The tensions between metropolitan hubs and provincial heartlands or between national plutocracies and globalist techno-utopians will not end in an economic equilibrium. Rather, the struggle with mercantilist China is likely to require new models and strategies for the West and its worldwide allies. In an important essay published in 2019, the academics Robert Atkinson and Michael Lind discuss five schools of political economy that are available to the US and, by extensive adaptation, to other Western countries: global neoliberalism, global libertarianism, progressive localism, national protectionism and national developmentalism.[3] Neoliberal and libertarian models are summarily dismissed as failed experiments, especially since the 'end of history'

Political and policy programme

utopias of the 1990s and 2000s that brought about the
dystopian consequences of the 2010s: deindustrialization, mass immigration and a new techno-managerial
class alongside disparities of power, wealth and status.
Progressive localism is described by Atkinson and Lind
as having enduring appeal because it draws on the
Jeffersonian tradition of a decentralized economy in
which only self-reliant small farms and firms can forge
a democratic polity based upon 'yeoman republican
virtue'. But behind the bold opposition to big business
lies – so contend the authors – an old, discredited
ideology of Keynesian redistribution from rich to poor,
massive state intervention in the market to break up
all large corporations and large-scale immigration to
diversify an otherwise ageing population.

Like localism, protectionism in its right-libertarian or
left-progressive variants has popular support on account
of immigration restrictions, high tariffs and a different
role of government: either a small federal government
with limited taxes and light-touch regulation or an
interventionist government with substantial investment
in infrastructure and skills. But protectionist walls will
not rebuild a nation's industrial and manufacturing base
capable of competing with the likes of China. Neither
tariffs nor import substitution is sufficient when protectionism will also undermine competitiveness by cutting
off global supply chains, barring entry to highly skilled
immigrants and hollowing out the role of the state as a
significant agent of economic development.

It is here that Atkinson and Lind make the case
for national developmentalism, which they define as
follows:

> Local communities are important, but in the modern
> world military security and economic efficiency can be

secured only by national economies anchored by large corporations. [...] a strong nation-state can moderate conflicts among workers and capitalists, in the interest of national economic strategy with military security and widespread prosperity as its objectives. The national developmentalist school views the big firms that can marshal the scale needed to compete as critical national resources. For this reason, the national developmentalist school extends a cautious welcome to efficient global oligopolies, American and foreign, as long as they are genuinely private corporations and not de facto agencies of foreign governments.[4]

As Atkinson and Lind point out, national developmentalism is not about pulling up the drawbridge, nor about neglecting the regionalization of trade, nor about ignoring the importance of integration in the global economy based on multinational supply chains. Rather, the difference that sets it apart from the other four schools is the central role of the state in championing national economic interests at home and abroad.

In policy terms, this means, first, building institutions such as regional or sector banks, research and development agencies and technology clusters to support state corporations and private companies to compete in the global economy, and, second, boosting productivity and real wages for workers in the national economy. It translates into an activist state that promotes research, innovation and investment in strategic sectors, using a mix of industrial policy, public finance for R&D and partnerships with businesses both small and large. Yet just as Covid-19 has strengthened the case for such models of government intervention, so too the latent danger of state/market-backed oligopolies at the expense of small- and medium-sized enterprises or local enterprise looms large.

Political and policy programme

In partial defence of national developmentalism, it rejects one-size-fits-all models. Instead, its advocates argue for a selective approach that views government as the champion of the country's common good, breaking with the liberal-libertarian dogma of enforcing rules for transactions between self-interested individuals in a free global market. 'To succeed in a multipolar world in which nations as well as firms compete for global market shares, we do not need to choose among liberty, prosperity, and power,' conclude Atkinson and Lind. 'National developmentalism, if done right, can give us all three.'[5]

Up to a point, theirs is a convincing vision, grounded in historical traditions and contemporary realities. As globalization slows down and fragments, countries require greater resilience to technological disruption, hostile foreign powers practising predatory state capitalism and shocks such as periodic financial crises or pandemics. Besides post-war Germany, Japan or South Korea, the US and the UK had developmental states for much of the period from the Second World War to the 1970s. The federal government promoted US businesses such as AT&T, RCA, IBM, GE and Xerox to build up economic capacity at home and compete successfully for market shares in the world economy. In a Cold War context, the 'military–industrial' complex with its dual military–civilian use of new technologies yielded enhanced innovation at the service of national security and shared prosperity. After the Sputnik wake-up call, the US substantially expanded federal spending on R&D to help it achieve technological domination over the USSR and globally.

In the UK, Labour won power in 1945 and 1950 based on programmes of national economic development. Conservative governments also adopted versions of

124

economic patriotism, as the historian David Edgerton has shown.[6] What he and Tom Nairn call a 'developmental state' was at the heart of rebuilding Britain following the devastation of the Second World War. Government and the free, democratic labour movement were key in domesticating capital and forging alliances with business at the service of national prosperity. Instead of class war or labour's surrender to capital, the Attlee government set the path for what Gramsci calls a national popular politics: a convergence of national with popular interests. Labour, according to Edgerton, stood 'not for class and nation but for class-in-nation; or more exactly, for nation over class'.[7] If Britain wants to prosper in the wake of both Brexit and Covid, then going forward the national interest will have to prevail over ideology or sectional interests.

But national developmentalism focused on the central state and big business alone will not suffice. To create a more resilient and secure society, Western countries – chief of all the US and the UK – need a model of political economy that rethinks the national economy in relation to local and regional levels. Industrial policy can no longer privilege large cities built on finance and real estate or exclusively on the high-productivity trading sectors. Nor can we expect wealth to trickle down from those working in high-value service jobs to those in low-productivity manual jobs. This not only ignores the diversity of regions and localities but also perpetuates the disparities of power, wealth and status that coincide with divisions along the lines of geography, age and education.[8]

Missing from national developmentalism is a concern for the civic infrastructure required to support research and innovation across the whole economy, not simply high-performing firms – an institutional ecology in which all parts of the country can develop and flourish, including small towns as well as rural and coastal areas. Shared prosperity will not happen based on a divided economy in which growing inequalities of wages, productivity and job security persist. A holistic approach is needed to bind together the pursuit of wealth, health and well-being. National developmentalism glosses over two dimensions that are critical to building relational and resilient economies. The first is what Karel Williams and other economists call the 'foundational economy' – the everyday economy on which lives and livelihoods depend.[9] The second is tackling head on the threat from big business, especially global corporations and tech monopolies, to the ecosystem of national, regional and local economic activity.[10]

The foundational economy

The 'everyday economy' shifts the emphasis from the global economy or central structures at the national level to those economic sectors made up of services, production and social goods that sustain our daily lives: retail, the food industry, hospitality, as well as manual jobs such as in construction, security or care. This part of the economy is characterized by low wages, low productivity and low skills, which prevent strong growth and human flourishing. Addressing these structural failures is key to a programme of national renewal that can generate shared prosperity for the whole country. Building the foundational economy that determines the well-being of most people is critical for ideas such as a 'universal basic infrastructure', which would ensure that all parts of a country have access to adequate housing, transport, education, health and social care.[11] Without firm foundations – work, family and local community – no economy can provide sufficient investment in infrastructure, decarbonize energy generation, support manufacturing and industry, unlock long-term investment and thereby enable growth across the nation. In turn, work, family and local communities can only be sustained over time by a 'universal basic infrastructure' embedded in relationships and institutions.

The key insight of this idea is that the foundations of wealth and value creation are being undermined in ways that harm all of us except perhaps the top few per cent in society. Cleaners, carers, rubbish collectors, nurses, shop workers and those picking crops are among the forgotten people of our economy. Their hard work is neither properly rewarded nor recognized and their meagre pay means that they struggle to make ends meet. A steady flow of migrant labour has reinforced the exploitation of workers, both indigenous and immigrant, while the top managers and their shareholders extract rents – excessive profits that far exceed value creation. This rentier capitalism destroys a market economy in which everybody has a chance to get their fair share.[12] Growing affluence for the few coincides with greater division and injustice. The price we pay for greater freedom of choice is higher levels of loneliness and social fragmentation.

Faced with this threat to the foundations of our economy and society, a focus on the infrastructure of everyday life can define an ambitious programme of national renewal. The emphasis has to be on work, wages, the place where people live and the wider civic infrastructure that supports small- and medium-sized businesses. Work – both paid and unpaid – is by far the most important question. To uphold the dignity of labour, our economy has to create value based on work that provides both income and meaning. Job losses and unemployment are drivers of precarity, poverty, ill health and death. A postliberal programme therefore needs to be built around a Jobs Guarantee – a programmatic policy that can act as an anchor.

During the last recession in 2009, the UK Labour government introduced the Future Jobs Funds, which tried to help the long-term unemployed back into employment. Faced with the prospect of mass unemployment in the wake of the Covid-19 pandemic, a Jobs Guarantee should be put in place, funded by government and implemented regionally and locally together with businesses and trade unions as well as universities or technical colleges. Such an initiative would provide employment to the long-term unemployed, either filling an existing vacancy or doing an apprenticeship or accredited training. Each activity offered under this scheme would be paid at least at the rate of the real living wage or the union-negotiated level. Priority should be given to jobs that help with post-Covid recovery and resilience – especially those in health and social care but also roles for other 'key workers', as well as jobs that offer a community or public benefit or help to decarbonize the economy. Key to the success of a Jobs Guarantee is to provide an enduring option of a job paid at a decent wage. It would help to eliminate the reserve army of unemployed and permanently change the balance of power in the labour market and economy.

A Jobs Guarantee also requires a recognition that the minimum wage as currently defined is not enough to honour the dignity of labour. Workers deserve the 'living wage' or even the 'family wage' in order to be able to feed themselves and their loved ones. Dignity in the workplace, which is vital for productivity and people's sense of self-worth, can be enhanced by stronger rights to collective bargaining and worker representation on both company boards and their remuneration committees. Drawing on the Jubilee campaign in favour of debt forgiveness, we need a popular movement to change corporate governance and reshape it to improve accountability, develop the knowledge and leadership of the workforce and embed capital within relationships and places.

New models of trade union organization in the 'gig economy' are desperately needed. Other examples include new Royal Colleges for carers, cooks, cleaners and security guards to improve employment conditions and raise the status of these sectors. A more balanced economy that values different talents can be built by creating a high-quality system of vocational training and through-life education offered by a new partnership between employers, trade unions and local government. These policies will only be able to serve the goals of shared prosperity and flourishing if they are embedded in a proper foundational economy with strong institutions and social relations of reciprocal trust and cooperation.

Rebalancing the economy

Covid-19 has shone a light on the unravelling of the everyday economy, which has been ravaged by the forces of global capitalism – especially technology and finance – and decimated by deindustrialization and the neglect of successive governments. Britain's economic model can be conceptualized as a Thatcherite mix of a low-tax, high-finance Singapore-on-Thames, combined with Keynesian state spending to 'level up' the 'left behind' parts of the country that look like the Eastern Germany of old. To which we must add the new vision of Taiwan-on-Trent: an activist, entrepreneurial state that supports technology-intensive industries and relies on exporting services to compete in the global economy. But such a strategy exacerbates the economic insecurity facing many communities. Free-trade deals and a top-down interventionist state will continue to concentrate wealth and power even as new elites purge the old establishment. Rebuilding will require a break with three underlying conditions: the centralization of power, the concentration of wealth as well as the commodification of our daily lives and our common home of nature. A more resilient, relational economy rests on government, business and trade unions working together for the common good. Shared prosperity depends on open, competitive markets anchored in institutions of innovation rather than the closed system of oligopolies and the total domination of tech platforms – and that is before they have acquired the power of mastering robotics and Artificial Intelligence.

For the foundational economy to survive and thrive, what is required beyond the political economy of national developmentalism is a strategy to take on the monopoly capitalism and the rentier economy. The tech corporations such as Facebook, Google and Amazon dominate not just the economy but also our democracy by controlling access to information and knowledge and by influencing public political debate. Facebook's dealings with Cambridge Analytica are just the tip of a giant iceberg that could sink competitive markets and democratic self-government. Today monopolistic capitalism resembles an 'empire of everything' that is as omnipresent as it is invisible – from the most global plane to the most local shop and high street.[13] It is destroying the everyday economy on which our prosperity and well-being depend.

Competition policy, especially in the UK, needs to be guided not merely by considerations of efficiency or even consumer welfare but rather by a commitment to value creation, a reconciliation of estranged interests between different stakeholders as well as a balance of domestic and foreign ownership – linked to obligations towards local places, people and the nation as a whole. The latter is particularly true for internet giants that exploit their workers and shirk their responsibility to pay tax commensurate with their business activities. National regulation alone will not resolve the hegemony of tech platform within and across countries.[14] Nor will it do to leave in place oligarchic 'empires of everything' and wait for market-based solutions. And nationalisation would merely transfer ownership at the top without necessarily improving the lot of workers, suppliers and the communities where the online behemoths operate.

The challenge before us is to turn the existing platforms into public utilities owned by the people, not the state, and to run them as mutuals – with private providers competing on the provision of services. Mutualizing the technological infrastructure is a way of learning the lesson from the limits of anti-trust action in the twentieth century, when private conglomerates like Standard Oil were broken up but over time oligopolies formed to restrict competition once more. By endowing assets in perpetuity to people, mutualization transfers the ownership of critical infrastructure away from the central state and the free market. Besides boosting the powers of the Competition and Markets Authority, the institutional foundations necessary for this model include the creation of an independent Office for Strategic Economic Assets that would be directly accountable to Parliament and invested with the authority to support the nation's critical infrastructure – including energy, aviation, arms producers and all the medical supplies neglected for decades.

Both the foundational and the national economy will only grow if they are re-endowed with an ecosystem of capital provision and local knowledge embodied in institutions. Another anchor of a postliberal economic policy is the establishment of regional and sector banks, constrained to lend within specific regions and sectors that are currently lacking in capital. Germany's system of *Landesbanken*, or regional banks, is one example, and there are two more pillars of the German model worthy of careful consideration: *Sparkassen* (credit unions) and the *Kreditanstalt für Wiederaufbau* (*KfW*). These three institutions are key to channelling capital to firms: *Sparkassen* operate locally and mostly finance local businesses, whereas the *Landesbanken* operate regionally and serve medium-sized enterprises. Crucially, the *KfW* is Germany's national development bank and finances large companies. In many cases, representatives from these three institutions play a role in the corporate governance of German businesses. Beyond the National Infrastructure Bank launched by the Chancellor of the Exchequer in the UK's March 2021 budget aimed at tilting finance to the north, a National Development Bank is necessary to join up Britain's lopsided financial system. Such an institution for the nation can also be used to invest in technology and knowledge, pooling the risks and sharing the rewards. For technological advances and knowledge-based innovation are a shared inheritance, part of the commons and a source of collective agency.[15]

In conclusion: national economic development built on the everyday economy is an old idea whose time has come again. It means putting work first through a Jobs Guarantee and paying the real 'living wage' or even the 'family wage'. It means strengthening workers' participation through renewed trade unions and workers' presence on company boards. It means recognizing the status of 'key workers' and their activity through the creation of new royal colleges, combined with new institutions for vocational and technical training. It means turning closed oligarchic systems into open, competitive markets by transforming tech platforms into public utilities. It means setting up regional and sectoral banks to spread capital investment across the forgotten parts of the economy, as well as creating a National Development Bank to provide finance to producers rather than rentiers who simply extract excessive profits. Focusing on the nation requires government and a civic ecology of institutions to serve the interests of future generations, and prioritize long-term development and resilience.

11

Renewing democratic corporatism

Hope for a more democratic future cannot rest on unforeseen crises that undermine the dominant ideologies of our age. Nor should societies place all their faith in protective states. Adjusting laws in times of crisis, as we have seen during the pandemic, can harden into new norms after the emergency has ended.[1] Unmeditated state sovereignty risks authoritarian coercion at home and anarchic chaos abroad – a Hobbesian war of all against all, as Christopher Lasch feared. Instead of returning to the neoliberal politics of the past, or seeking comfort in authoritarian nationalism, societies should look to democratic corporatism as a model for the political future. To protect citizens from the pressures of both state and market power, the intermediary institutions that help constitute society need to be strengthened. These include trade unions, universities, local authorities, business associations, faith communities, as well as other places of exchange and association, such as bars and bank branches, cafés and civic halls, restaurants and sport clubs. Such institutions pluralize state and market, thereby upholding democracy against a concentration of capital or bureaucracy. Only by renewing democratic pluralism will societies achieve greater social solidarity and humanity.

A corporatist polity

In Britain and other Western countries, the response to Covid-19 has already inspired a new impetus to corporatist bargaining between the state, business, trade unions and the charitable sector – negotiating state subsidy of wages and emergency loans to both companies and charities. But this new corporatism depends too much on the will of the executive and on central government resources, and not enough on a decentralized form of democracy. A corporatist polity is meant to constrain state and market power within a balanced institutional arrangement. That requires the devolution of resources and power across the country, not just the delegation of responsibilities to city-regions which in the critical fight against the pandemic lacked authority and depended on central government funds. Covid-19 has shone a cold light on just how broken Britain's overcentralized unitary state is compared with the more corporatist polities of Germany or South Korea.

Here there are lessons to be learned from the post-war settlement for the renewal of democratic corporatism today. First of all, the new individual rights after the Second World War were linked to corresponding duties and obligations, based on the principle of reciprocity not only between citizen and state but also among citizens across classes and generations. Britain's welfare state as originally envisioned by William Beveridge was founded on the idea of mutual insurance, which the working class and the labour movement had pioneered

135

since the middle of the nineteenth century. Accordingly, welfare benefits rested on the notion of rewards received for contribution to society – mainly through work but also the war effort, which depended so critically on women working in factories and caring for the injured. The former Labour MP Frank Field puts this well: 'Beveridge saw his welfare proposals as a means of moulding an active, independent citizenry that practised the virtues of hard work, honesty and prudence. His fundamental principle was that receipt of welfare was to be dependent on what a person had paid into the scheme.'[2] The post-war welfare state grew out of the solidarity experienced during two world wars and reflected a sense of national belonging to a plural polity composed of corporate bodies.

Second, the practice of reciprocity characterized relations both within and across countries.[3] The institutions of Bretton Woods conceived by John Maynard Keynes helped to constrain global capital and directed it to largely productive activities as the peoples of the West began the process of reconciliation and reconstruction. After the slide into protectionism and nationalism during the interwar period and the Great Depression, the new settlement sought to balance fairer trade with a measure of 'mutual protectionism': sheltering agriculture, coal and steel as well as other critical industries from cut-throat competition and the great power politics of the nascent Cold War confrontation. Catholic social thought, with its emphasis on a 'third way' between totalitarian state communism and *laissez-faire* free-market capitalism, played a decisive role in forging both Christian and social democracy on the European continent.

Third, the post-1945 order really did chart an alternative to both individualism and statism by developing

136

a corporatist settlement in a more plural direction.[4] This involved a negotiated compromise between groups of society rather than a contractual agreement among individuals (as for liberals) or a diktat imposed by the central state (as for technocratic Fabian-style planning). These groups were not only government and business but also organized labour, which included the trade unions but also the cooperative movement (both of which were influenced by various Christian traditions, not least non-conformists). These corporate bodies came to agreements on working conditions, wage bargaining and employment standards – a process facilitated by government but without the use of state coercion. Plural corporatism took the form of reconciling estranged interests, with both business and the unions being given greater economic duties towards their members and society at large in exchange for more political influence.

Fourth, there was a marked difference between the federal polities of Germany and the US, on the one hand, and the more centralized unitary states of post-war Britain and France – even if the latter has always been less capitalistic than its ally across the Channel or the Atlantic. In the German and American cases, a vast array of civil associations and corporate bodies contributed both to the political process and to economic decision-making. A blend of more virtuous elites and greater popular participation (compared with the interwar period and post-1980s new settlement) ensured a degree of economic democracy. Yet it must be stressed that Germany's model of a social market economy with co-decision and worker representation on company boards owed much to the work of people like Allan Flanders, a former Oxford economist and democratic socialist who, together with other British civil servants working in post-war Germany, designed many of the institutions – including a vocational labour market model in relation to craft and the banking system based upon regional and sectoral endowment.[5]

Today many of these institutions are needed to help with Britain's national renewal anchored in the political and civic inheritance of self-governing institutions. The impact of the pandemic shows how both the body politic and the national economy require a transformation that links growth and productivity to the skill, knowledge and character of the workforce. That involves not just a rebalancing between Higher Education and Further Education but also a profound renewal of universities and vocational and technical training colleges – many of which lack autonomy, ethos and genuine excellence.

At the same time, Covid-19 foreshadows a new corporatist settlement. Government, business, the trade unions and charities all came together to bargain and agree on the job retention scheme and emergency loans to non-state institutions. Civil society organizations and mutual aid societies have stepped in to provide critical support for agriculture, health, welfare and mental health. We have witnessed the beginnings of a revival of corporate bodies and reciprocal bonds.[6]

Yet faced with the forces of global capitalism and technology, no country can do this on its own. Democratic and plural associations are also needed internationally to enable workers to resist the dehumanization and exploitation of the world economy. The alternative to hyper-capitalism and authoritarian nationalism is a renewed democratic corporatism that can combine a protective state with international cooperation to serve the common good.

For this reason, we require cross-border, rather than merely national, restrictions on globalization. A

renewed model of democratic corporatism can potentially outflank both US free-market fundamentalism
and Chinese state capitalism. A good start would be
to expand corporatist bargaining at national levels
between the state, business, trade unions and the
charitable sector. Governments should champion cross-
border deals that link workers and civic groups, thereby
protecting them from the homogenizing pressures of
state and market power. This could be partially achieved
via a commitment to pay workers of international
businesses the 'living wage' of the country where they
work – especially in the most precarious sectors such as
care, cleaning and delivery.

Together with regional authorities and local
government, national leaders should also support the
reform of trade unions to give workers proper representation (especially in under-unionized sectors) and to
promote workplace democracy – including for those
working in multinational corporations. Internationally,
cooperation between democratic nations needs to
include a certain amount of required fiscal parity in
order to restrain the urge to attract the most unscru-
pulous international operations. Without this carapace,
individual countries on their own will not be able
to resist the lure of global capitalism and the tech
oligarchy.

Could the EU renew its corporatist tradition?

It is here that organizations such as the EU have to
renew their own best traditions. The more Catholic
and Protestant dimension of the EU's founding legacy
has always linked subsidiarity with federalism at every
level, refusing *either* the absolutist nation-state *or* an

international technocracy. In the face of both liberal globalization and national populism, this 'third way' needs to be recovered. To build such a model, the EU requires a radical rethink, which must shift its core purpose away from predominantly serving the interests of capital aided and abetted by a regulatory state that seeks to maximize consumer welfare instead of pursuing the common good.

Based on a fusion of Thatcherite economics and the Napoleonic Code, the Single European Act of 1985, which created the Single Market, privileged the four freedoms of capital, people, goods and services at the expense of the principles of solidarity and subsidiarity. By favouring the market over society, the European project abandoned the legacy of Catholic social teaching and mutualism. Even after the end of the lockdown, some restrictions on the free movement of people will likely remain in place. The same should apply to capital, so that national companies are safe from takeovers by multinationals which strip assets by outsourcing operations, load debt onto balance sheets and further empower shareholders at the expense of workers, suppliers and the communities where businesses operate.

But Brussels must go much further in curtailing financial speculation and instead channel capital into productive activities. One vehicle could be the post-Covid Recovery Fund, worth €750 bn, with member states issuing common debt to fund about 70 per cent (over €500 bn) worth of grants to help those countries that have been hit hardest by the pandemic. Another way to do this would be to create new bonds for capital investment issued by national, regional and even municipal bodies, but underwritten by all member states in order to pool risk. The issuance of such bonds should be linked to devolving tax-and-spend powers to lower levels of government, including that of the state, thereby reducing the size and costs of the central bureaucracy. Such an idea would likely be opposed by the 'frugal four' – Austria, Denmark, Sweden and the Netherlands – and maybe by Germany and Finland too. But this was assumed about the now approved Recovery Fund too. It sets an important precedent on which other reforms and policies can be built in future.

For such a plan to work, the north of Europe likely needs to accept a measure of debt forgiveness for the southern nations, but in ways that do not hurt individual savers – even if taxpayers as a whole would take a hit. And then the EU needs to try to craft a better trading balance of internal exports and imports that could release both the southern countries and the German populace from the negative effects of the German imbalance towards exporting. These effects include permanent deficits in the South and lower than living wages in the North. Over time, the imbalances will impinge on Germany's living standards and trigger political opposition. This dire prospect helps support the case for radical reform.

Clearly that needs to be accompanied by a more shared, democratic and politically integrated management of the euro, if that currency survives in its current configuration. At the same time, the EU could deploy its trans-state authority to encourage in every nation a reinvigoration of local government, regional banking and the growth of personal savings and assets. These processes are capable of inhibiting the rise of debt dependency and the consequent erosion of personal and community self-government at the hands of impersonal financial and bureaucratic power.

A more corporatist EU would also go a long way towards allowing state aid for manufacturing and industry to be more flexible. If a competitive market is the aim, then groups of countries such as the EU have to be allowed to support domestic businesses against state-backed conglomerates from China or multi-billion hedge funds from the US. Another European response could be not just to impose fines on uncompetitive actions by behemoths such as Microsoft or Google, but also to adopt laws that turn online oligarchic platforms into public utilities, as the previous chapter suggested. And as the French President Emmanuel Macron has suggested, Europe – which can mean the EU plus European partners such as the UK – has to build its own solutions in order not to depend on American or Chinese technologies.[7] His argument is both economic and ethical – saying that European-owned and -developed telecommunications ensure better security of information and the defence of citizens' right to privacy.

Currently the EU is a long way off such a capability. The problem is that the current agents of Keynesian reform, whether they are businesses or bureaucracies, have themselves become totally imbued with merely profit-seeking and instrumentally controlling habits of mind. We need, therefore, new institutional agents of change. But rather than unrealistically beginning from nothing, the EU member states and other governments in Europe should encourage corporate bodies to behave more virtuously and with greater social purpose. A mutualist ethos can be encouraged through regulation, preferential treatment and higher requirements of vocational training and professional belonging.

Among European leaders, Macron comes closest to defining such a vision:

> Europe is not just a market. For decades, we have acted implicitly as if Europe were a single market. But we have not conceived Europe internally as a finite

142

political space. Our currency is not finished. Until this summer's agreements, we did not have a real budget and real financial solidarity. We have not entirely thought through all the social issues that make us a united space. And we have not sufficiently thought about what makes us a power in the concert of nations: a highly integrated region with a clear political given. Europe must rethink itself politically and act politically to define common objectives that are more than merely delegating our future to the market.[8]

The Covid-induced cataclysm should rule out a return to the ideological status quo before populism. Both the EU and the US under President Biden will have to break with the technocratic centrism that created the conditions for the populist insurgency while also fending off the revolutionary left. Democratic corporatism, underpinned by a pluralism that focuses on the dignity of the person, can help chart a new settlement: a politics and an economics of the common good.

12

Reweaving the social fabric

Bourgeois order in decline

What can we learn from the French writer Michel Houellebecq? He is typically dismissed as a right-wing reactionary misogynist who indulges in nostalgic nihilism and fantasises about sexual orgies. Yet for all the crude, graphic depictions of sex, Houellebecq's novels offer a diagnosis of the bourgeoisie in decline across themes such as tourism, technology, terrorism, routinized jobs, addiction to anti-depressants, internet pornography and, yes, compulsive sexuality. What he anatomizes more acutely than perhaps any other contemporary Western writer is the disintegration of the bourgeois social order: middle-class norms of loyalty, faithfulness, self-restraint, joy, festivity and hope. Instead, much of the bourgeoisie today is mired in a mix of betrayal, infidelity, excess, sadness, boredom and despair. As the American author Christopher Caldwell has remarked,

> Certain basic things that important novelists do, Houellebecq does not. Great novels usually concern the relationships, institutions, and ideals out of which the 'bourgeois' social order is knit together – marriages, schools, jobs, piety, patriotism. But in our time,

relationships fail to take root. Institutions fall apart. The visible social order seems not to be the real one.[1]

Houellebecq neither glorifies the old order, nor does he judge the 'losers' of the new meritocracy. Instead of taking sides, he explores the growing polarization of a culture that has lost its ethical moderation to extreme opposites that fuel each other: left-liberal cultural liberation from familial constraints on desire that end up championing right-liberal economic liberation from communal constraints on capital because both are grounded in individualism and liberty reduced to the unfettered autonomy of private choice. Or consider the stand-off between liberalism and populism in his most controversial novel, *Submission*, and the slide into new forms of fascism. At the heart of Houellebecq's writings is the sense of irretrievable cultural and institutional loss – illustrated by the loss of true love. In each of his novels, there is a woman – Christiane in *Atomised* (aka *The Elementary Particles*), Camille in Houellebecq's latest novel, *Serotonin* – who could have been a wife, a mother, a soulmate with whom the protagonist might have built a more meaningful life.

Houellebecq is far from alone in highlighting the complex emotions of rage and despair, anger and alienation that characterize contemporary communities across the West. In his remarkable book *Radical Hope: Ethics in the Face of Cultural Devastation*, Jonathan Lear explores some of these issues by asking whether it is even possible to offer hope after the death of a particular culture.[2] More than the disappearance of certain practices, cultural devastation leads to a void in which there is no sense of what the good life might be – or whether life itself has any meaning at all. If the social fabric is torn asunder and the culture of everyday existence is irretrievably lost, then how can we refer to any shared cultural customs? What binds us together across generations when, as Lear puts it, 'culture does not tend to train the young to endure its own breakdown'?[3] His answer is that rebuilding social ties where precious few or none exist requires re-imagining a common future by avoiding despair and the fatalism of inevitable decline. Communities, however broken, have traditions embedded in institutions and civic practices that can offer some hope.

Community spirit

Recent events testify to this. In individualistic cultures such as the UK or the US, the Covid-19 crisis has revealed both the material disintegration of society and the deep desire for spiritual community: the spirit of togetherness and shared social practice. On the one hand, the sheer extent of social isolation and communal fragmentation has become more apparent. As people were confined to their homes and neighbourhoods, many discovered just how little they knew about those who live next door and how frayed our social fabric is. According to a 2016 study by the British Red Cross and the Co-op, over 9 million – nearly a fifth of the total UK population – say that they are always or often lonely, but almost two-thirds feel uncomfortable speaking about it.[4] Many of them are over seventy years old and so in the cohort of those who are having to shield. The viral pandemic has thrown a new light on loneliness. The lockdown and the limbo we found ourselves in until a vaccine was rolled out turned it into a social pandemic.

On the other hand, the popular response to restrictions has led to a revival of community spirit. From

WhatsApp chats to Covid-19 Mutual Aid groups, and from over 700,000 volunteers for the NHS to countless acts of communal solidarity, people have formed local initiatives that tie in with larger-scale hub-and-spoke networks – sharing ideas and providing concrete support to some of the most isolated and vulnerable members of society. Relationships offline – whether at home or 'socially distanced' – have taken on a renewed significance even as we moved much of our work and shopping online. However, we realized more acutely after Covid than before Covid that technological connectivity is no substitute for social connections. There is BC and then there is AC.

The paradox of liberal individualism is that we end up being at once more connected and more fragmented. Pope Francis puts this well: 'The pandemic has exposed the paradox that while we are more connected, we are also more divided. Feverish consumerism breaks the bonds of belonging.'[5] Covid-19 opens up the space for renewing a communitarian spirit of rediscovering the importance of attachment and affection for particular people and places. Protective isolation has thrown us back onto family and neighbourhood, community and country. Yet at the same time, we find greater meaning in virtual connections worldwide, crossing liberal fault lines between the private and the public, the local and the global. Binding together the tension between being embedded in places and being connected across the planet is our yearning for purpose: a natural desire for relationships and institutions that provide meaning. If humans are meaning-seeking and story-telling animals, then the self only makes sense in something greater than itself. In our quest for a purposeful life, we discern at the heart of ourselves what the late Jonathan Sacks, former UK chief rabbi, calls the greater human 'we', all the covenantal ties binding us together as humans who are social beings.[6]

Covenantal ties renewed

Covenant – the complex web of intergenerational bonds – is more primary than contract because relationships matter more than transactions. Humans need love, lived solidarity and emotional stability as much as physical or material security, like shelter or money to put food on the table. Being born into a state of complete dependency, we are embodied creatures who are oriented towards our mother, family and extended kin who provide the love we need to live and flourish. Rites of passage into adulthood involve life in society with a balance of rights and obligations. First there is 'we', then there is 'me'.

Beyond wealth and power, humans tend to seek mutual recognition: valuing everyone's talents, vocations and contribution to society. Connected with this is our natural disposition for what George Orwell termed honourable performance. We take pride in a job well done. The forging of a common life between separate selves who are also relational beings requires a politics based on a transcendent conversation, which can address deeper divisions around questions of shared belonging. Paradoxically, the search for the self leads us to discover the priority of the relational over the purely individual or collective.

The pandemic has exposed just how vulnerable our lives are. From the 'wet markets' of Wuhan and the cheap flights that carried this virus across the globe, to the locking down of countries and the crashing of economies, we have seen our fragile systems collapse.

In one sense, the deadly disease has threatened all of us, everywhere and simultaneously. Faced with our own frailty, we have been forced to confront existential questions about life and mortality. In another sense, the Covid-19 crisis is not the 'great leveller' at all. It has affected groups very differently, disproportionately hitting minority communities, those in precarious jobs, the elderly and people of all ages with underlying health conditions. Far from changing everything, the pandemic has accelerated and amplified disparities of power, wealth and social status that have developed for decades.

Those worst hit face greater economic interdependence but also greater social isolation than before. As the bonds of family, community, work, church and nation have declined, the scale of loneliness and seclusion is growing. Many of us are connected with one another online, but often we lack real relationships in the places we inhabit. The social theorist Sherry Turkle has called this paradoxical phenomenon 'alone together'.[7] With new levels of digital dependence and addictive attention-seeking, over-excitement and disenchantment cascade into each other. Instead of mutual recognition and flourishing anchored in notions of the common good, politics and social life become debased. Our selves are individualized identity or part of some collective mob – as painfully visible in the violent rioting by both revolutionary left and far-right groups following the brutal murder of George Floyd.

From dystopia to hope

The global wave of protests after the imposition of the global lockdown underscores the limits of liberalism. As optimism gives way to pessimism even among ardent progressives, the utopian dream of liberal progress has not survived contact with the reality of our contingent existence. As John Gray has remarked, whatever we gain in advancement can just as quickly be reversed.[8] Hyper-mobility begets enforced isolation, just as mass unemployment returns after the latest stock market boom and bust. The forces of progress, such as global capitalism or disruptive technology, have morphed into engines of regression.

But it is not just liberalism's faith in a better future that finds itself on the 'wrong side of history'. Long-held assumptions about human nature are also in question. The liberal idea – already articulated by Thomas Hobbes and John Locke – that we are solitary selves bound to one another by contract based on enlightened self-interest is an abstraction from practical life and from people's personal and existential concerns. Even liberals like John Stuart Mill could see the limits of utilitarian liberalism: in a memorable phrase, Mill characterized Bentham's philosophy as the empiricism of 'one who has had little experience'.[9] What is in question is liberal anthropology. Far from being selfish, greedy and distrustful of others, many of us are capable of solidarity and generosity vis-à-vis our neighbours, who not so long ago were often utter strangers. In the immediate aftermath of the Covid-19 outbreak, people came together in groups to help their communities fight the pandemic by delivering food and medicine to those self-isolating at home. By contrast, liberal culture oscillates between selfishness and abstract altruism, forgetting the fellow-feeling that has been manifest in countless acts of generosity across the land.

By preferring private autonomy to fraternity and self-emancipation to common endeavour, the utopia of liberalism has dystopian effects. It has brought about in practice the social fragmentation that the liberal commitment to individualism assumed in theory. Of those 9 million who report that they are always or often lonely, many are elderly people who feel abandoned and endure a state of permanent social distancing. It is not just during enforced isolation that liberalism's focus on choice and freedom rings hollow. Even in more normal times, the liberal mission of liberating the individual from all social constraints leaves us free yet fragile. By dismantling hierarchies and cultural ties, liberalism undermines the social fabric which binds people together and gives purpose to liberty: the relational and institutional support people need to sustain their deep desire for more community.

The virus has revealed just how removed liberal utopianism is from lived reality. Social distancing brings us closer to our immediate families, so often denigrated by left progressives. The lockdown has revived mutual aid and a sense of social solidarity across the nation, so frequently neglected by right-wing neoliberals. The limits of liberal individualism are even more evident than in the aftermath of the financial crash. We are forced into protective isolation that generates closer connections from our streets to the globe. Loyalty to local businesses and a generous disposition of give-and-receive re-emerge as more primary instincts than transactional trucking and trading or the fusion of state centralization with crony capitalism.[10]

The politics that commands popular support is one that reflects reality: our health; work in support of our communities; the love we have for family and friends. The pandemic reminds us of the paradox that is our human condition. We are experiencing at once frailty and resilience, fright and courage, helplessness and

151

extraordinary acts of sacrifice. Contemporary liberals have had little to say about these moral sentiments and social virtues. Without recovering the language of the common good, liberalism will neither renew itself nor offer real hope to people.

Policies for a new social covenant

A postliberal politics that does not slide into the antiliberal extreme of nationalism and neo-fascism is a politics that puts society before economics or coercion. It involves a plural, decentralized democracy that devolves power and resources to local communities: from local government – via intermediary institutions such as trade unions or chambers of commerce to reconcile the interests of capital and labour – to voluntary associations and new mutual groups. For example, civic groups involved in sustaining vital sectors such as agriculture, education, welfare and health need access to finance through the new national development bank and its regional representations. In a recent report commissioned by the UK government to look at 'sustaining the community spirit we saw during lockdown into the recovery phase and beyond', the Conservative MP Danny Kruger argues for a new Community Power Act, building a deliberative democracy, participatory budgets in local government and citizen assemblies to help 'create the plural public square we need'.[11] Elsewhere I have suggested a number of institutional reforms aimed at reviving democratic politics in regions and localities.[12] But beyond institutional reform, a number of policy changes are required to help reweave the torn social fabric.

One area for radical reform is family policy. The family – in all its plural forms – is the fundamental pillar of society. Yet right-wing libertarian and left-wing statist ideas have failed to support family formation and childrearing. By reducing family to an economic cost–benefit calculation, left and right reflect what the American feminist political philosopher Nancy Fraser has called the 'reactionary neoliberal' and 'progressive neoliberal' approaches to policy.[13] The postliberal alternative is to provide at once more universal and more particular, targeted support to all families. Specific policies include more generous parental leave – both maternity and paternity leave – and recognizing caring responsibilities in the tax system, as David Goodhart has argued, by allowing married couples and long-term cohabiters to pool their tax-free allowances. That would correct the 'couple penalty' in the benefits system and leave families with a single breadwinner with more of their earned income.

But the key policy to anchor a postliberal pro-family programme is the public provision of more generous childcare support that reflects social, cultural values and not just economic choices. In OECD countries, the average spending on child benefits is about 2 per cent of GDP, with the UK and Sweden at 3.5 per cent while the US commits a mere 0.6 per cent. This exposes the hypocrisy of those US politicians among Republicans or Democrats who profess to defend 'family values'. But more fundamentally, both left and right assume that raising children reduces labour market participation and should therefore be outsourced to state institutions or private organizations. Yet childrearing is work – work which makes a valuable contribution to society and which deserves dignity and recognition.[14] Childcare payment should take the form of either allowing parents to stay at home or paying for nurseries. At-home childcare supported by the benefits system will finally recognize all the unpaid work mostly mothers – and sometimes fathers – are doing. It could be used for communal childcare too, with relatives, friends or neighbours pooling their resources to care for each other's children.

Another key pro-family policy idea that postliberals should champion is support for extended families to provide social care. Both national resilience and inter-generational justice demand that countries such as the US and the UK introduce an adult social care system for all. So far, attempts to pay for the exponentially growing costs of social care have failed in the UK. This was clearly exemplified by the 2017 Conservative Party manifesto policy to force people to sell their real estate even in the case of long-term illness such as dementia – a promise that amounted to telling the British people 'lose your mind, lose your home', as Maurice Glasman put it.

A much better model is Germany's adult care insurance system created in 1995, which all working adults pay into. By pooling risk and combining personal contribution with public funding, the *Pflegeversicherung* has so far avoided astronomical costs and enjoys cross-party and popular support. As the British health think-tank the Nuffield Trust has remarked, the German model, despite various problems, has laid the 'foundations for a system that has been able to adapt and respond to changing circumstances'[15] – precisely what is necessary in the face of unprecedented events such as pandemics. Such a mutual insurance system can be modified to provide financial support for family members who want to care for their parents or grandparents but struggle to do so because they have to work full-time.

Building on the principle of contribution, Frank Field has developed policy ideas for 'a new welfare state run by three mutual insurance bodies controlling health, pensions and national insurance'. It is worth quoting him at some length:

> The first would take over existing national insurance benefits. The mutual structure would consist of a pot into which national insurance contributions would be paid. It would be responsible to the membership for its finances and levels of benefit paid.
>
> The second should cover the National Health Service. Health funding will remain in a state of long-term crisis until we establish a direct link between what individuals demand as potential patients and what they are prepared to pay for as contributors. A separate national health insurance contribution would begin to establish that link, but also give members a direct say over the kind of services they wish to pay for.
>
> Finally, [... a] pension system that reduces the need for means testing has considerable electoral appeal, until people realise that the government proposes to pay for it by pinching contributions from other contributors. So a third mutual entity should incorporate the National Employment Savings Trust, the pensions scheme set up by Labour in 2008. This should ensure that savings over the longer term guarantee a pension scheme with the funds to make payments above means-tested assistance levels. It would have the further benefit of encouraging pensioners to build up other savings to top up their state pension.[16]

If a political and popular consensus can be built for an insurance-based social care system, then this could be the starting point for a wider transformation of the welfare state along the lines proposed by Field. It would mean moving away from a centralized bureaucracy that ends up outsourcing public services to private providers and towards a more mutualized system with a greater element of personal contribution. The current system is broken: top-down, target-driven and based on payment by results, with efficiency and 'value for money' imposing a managerialist bureaucracy of Byzantine complexity that makes Whitehall simultaneously overcentralized and weak at the core. This logic wastes both money and people's resources, reducing citizens to administrative units while public sector workers are debased to impersonal cogs in a machine servicing an utterly impersonal system of key performance indicators, testing, assessing, auditing and tidal waves of forms, questionnaires, surveys and reports. Means testing is wasteful and humiliating whereas an insurance system honours contribution.

Part of the answer is a much more decentralized system based on contribution that offers people more scope to top up their coverage with private insurance while funding welfare institutions at both regional and local levels, thereby enabling them to respond to local problems and put in place more place- and people-based provision – whether test and trace or actual care. Contributory welfare within the national insurance model means that what people take out depends in large part on what they have put in. Unpaid work at home, mostly performed by women, would be recognized as a contribution that entitles people to receive rewards. Decentralization and contribution are principles around which we can link bottom-up, community-based solutions (care, welfare, training) to larger-scale models of delivery: for example, by bringing together voluntary associations and social enterprises under the guidance of the mayor, the assembly and local civil servants. In this manner, local government neither provides all public services itself nor outsources them all to the cheapest for-profit supplier but, instead, promotes more mutualist arrangements by connecting and coordinating different providers and participants who associate more freely with one another.[17]

A concrete example can be found in the London borough of Barking and Dagenham, one of Britain's most deprived and fastest-changing areas. It has persistently high levels of unemployment, a chronic lack of social housing, a significant increase in ghettoized estates, shocking levels of homelessness, as well as long-standing problems with teenage pregnancies, domestic violence and low life expectancy. In the 2010 general election, the incumbent MPs Margaret Hodge and Jon Cruddas fought off a strong challenge from the British National Party, who had previously won twelve council seats in the 2006 local elections. Today Barking and Dagenham are home to an extraordinary experiment in bridging broken communities and reweaving the social fabric. After defeating the fascism of the BNP, councillors knew that the old model of social paternalism would neither be feasible in an age of austerity for local government nor be desirable as it diminishes people's sense of agency and belonging. Instead of the old tired models, they worked with the Participatory City Foundation over five years and with £7 million of funding, supporting a new initiative, called 'Every One, Every Day', that is anchored in common principles of proximity to people, civic participation and place.

Concretely, the project does not require substantial time or any financial contribution from local residents. Instead, with council investment, it creates spaces for people by setting up physical infrastructure to improve everyday life: communal shops that had disappeared from the high street dominated by corporate chains; informal childcare arrangements run by mothers and carers. The commentator George Monbiot summarizes this well:

157

There are welcoming committees for new arrivals to the street, community potluck meals, cooking sessions and street lunches. There's a programme to turn boring patches of grass into community gardens, play corners and outdoor learning centres. There's a bee school and a chicken school (teaching urban animal husbandry), sewing and knitting sessions, places for freelance workers to meet and collaborate, computing and coding workshops, storytelling for children, singing sessions and a games café. A local football coach has started training people in the streets. There's a film studio and a DIY film festival too, tuition for spoken-word poets and a scheme for shutting streets to traffic so children can play after school. Local people have leapt on the opportunities the new system has created. There's a long way to go. Four thousand of the borough's 200,000 people have participated so far. But the rate of growth suggests it is likely to be transformative. The council told me the programme had the potential to reduce demand for social services as people's mental and physical health improves. Partly as a result, other boroughs and other cities are taking an interest in this remarkable experiment.[18]

As the example of Barking and Dagenham shows, the combined principles of contribution, participation and decentralized democracy can help to repair broken communities and begin to reweave the social fabric. The task is to build a new national covenant from neighbourhood to nation that creates a partnership between estranged interests, generations and regions. Based on institutions that uphold shared benefits and mutual obligations, it binds people into a common life anchored in the common good.

13

Restoring the common home
of nature

The economic scarring from Covid-19 is likely to be deep and long, as the worst contraction of output on record was temporarily cushioned by various government schemes to pay workers and provide emergency loans. But it will hit workers and businesses in a series of aftershocks that could be bigger than the original earthquake. Parallels have been drawn with the Great Depression of 1929–32 and the New Deal devised by President Franklin D. Roosevelt, who was widely referenced in Michael Gove's July 2020 Ditchley Lecture, where he sought to define the UK government's post-Covid mission.[1] One of the main planks of Roosevelt's New Deal was the creation of the Civilian Conservation Corps (CCC), which today serves as an example of how to fuse an economic with an ecological and ethical response to our crisis. Now, as then, one key task is to save millions of young people across the West from the scourge of unemployment while also helping the environment under threat from the forces of global capitalism and unrestrained technology.

As the economists Danny Blanchflower and David Bell argued, Roosevelt's CCC hired young, unmarried men to work on conservation and development of natural resources in rural areas. During its nine years of operation, 3 million young men, mainly aged 18 to 25, passed through the CCC. Most of the jobs were manual. It was credited with improving the employability, wellbeing and fitness of participants. Introducing a UK version of the CCC focused on mitigating climate change risks and aimed at those aged 16 to 24 could avoid the creation of yet another 'lost generation' [...]. It would build on the enthusiasm of the young to save the planet. There is no shortage of issues to address – flood risks, tree planting, domestic heating conversion, renewable energy, restoring biodiversity etc.[2]

National Nature Service

Invoking Roosevelt's creation of the CCC, a coalition of environmental groups has called on the UK government to establish a National Nature Service (NNS). This call is backed by over fifty organizations, including National Parks England, the RSPB, the Wildlife Trusts, the Woodland Trust, WWF, Friends of the Earth and Greenpeace, who together represent millions of members. Their compelling case rests on the funda-mental connections between the current viral and ecological crises. At its core lies health: the health of humankind and of nature. Nature depletion has left our countries vulnerable to the effects of pandemics and of climate change. In turn, medical and climate emergencies undermine the health and well-being of citizens, with millions of people unemployed or forced to shield at home – in particular, already disadvantaged groups and communities, who often have limited or no access to safe wild spaces nearby.

160

Besides an economic recovery, countries such as the US and the UK require a fairer, more resilient and ecologically balanced model of national development.

> These outcomes can be achieved together through a 'National Nature Service' (NNS): an employment and training scheme in which tens of thousands of jobseekers, particularly young people and those from underrepresented and disadvantaged groups, would be employed and trained in environmental projects designed to level up access to nature, address social and health inequalities and bend the curve on nature's decline.
>
> The scheme is inspired by the success of the 1930s US Civilian Conservation Corps and the 1970s UK Manpower Services Commission, but updated for the modern day and the UK context. The scheme would be funded across the UK by central government, including funding for devolved governments to run the scheme in their respective countries.[3]

Setting up an NNS would help with the regeneration of suburban, rural and coastal areas, which have borne the brunt of global finance capitalism, deindustrialization and the concentration of wealth in metropolitan areas. It would sustain the recovery of both the economy and nature, thereby supporting personal and collective well-being. With the appropriate investment in training and employment, people of all ages and backgrounds could participate in the work of natural renewal and thereby enjoy a greener, healthier and more prosperous future – linked to the Jobs Guarantee discussed in chapter 10.

The NNS initiative is backed by organizations representing a vast array of interests, from nature conservation to young people, from BAME communities to the creative arts. They all have lent their support to this idea, which brings together the public, private and voluntary sector around a common interest in ecological resilience and shared prosperity. The coalition of green groups has drawn up a list of 330 or so projects on which work can start immediately, such as flower meadows, 'tiny forests' in cities and hillside schemes to cut flooding, to which can be added flood defences, cleaning up riverbanks and helping British farmers. According to the advocates of the NNS, funding the projects and training workers would create 10,000 jobs and could be part of a green recovery from the coronavirus pandemic. They estimate that 200,000 hectares of habitat in both rural and coastal areas could be saved, offering better access to nature for many thousands of people and helping to reverse the decline in biodiversity at a cost of just £315 million.[4]

Of course, the climate emergency will require much more action at all levels, including international coordination to deal with emissions, halt the destruction of biodiversity and promote the development of green technology. But for environmental politics to succeed, it cannot remain purely aggregate and abstracted from people's place and their daily lives. Like economic, social and political reform, it has to be anchored in our everyday experience and link together different scales and levels: from the personal to the collective, and from the local to the global.

Global environmental change and national ecology

As with the economic recovery after Covid-19, the nation will be central in the fight against ecological devastation. Western countries have taken some steps to meet their carbon emission targets by 2030 and 2050, but the decisions so far are insufficient and likely to be cancelled out by new road construction and, in the case of the UK, the continuation of a fuel tax freeze. The Johnson government's announcement to prohibit the sale of new petrol and diesel cars by 2030 is welcome, but it is not supported by a joined-up approach to energy generation and the provision of charging portals for electric vehicles. The public spending on fighting climate change is a fraction of the Ministry of Defence's annual budget. This, combined with the focus on carbon-driven climate change rather than a holistic approach to the environment that seeks to reverse the catastrophic loss in biodiversity, suggests that green new deals backed by states and business are intended to help save capitalism from itself. Yet if we have learned one thing from the 2008 financial crash, it is that regulation alone will not transform the capitalist logic of commodifying labour, land and life.

Nor will an expanded welfare state be able to resolve on its own the fallout from the climate emergency. That is because welfarism is too centralized and too remote from people to organize collective action. While providing an important safety net, the welfare state often turns citizens into passive recipients rather than change agents. It is true, however, as the commentator Anatol Lieven argues, that enhanced social security and public healthcare are important in tackling the climate emergency, for three related reasons: first, to compensate – as centralized welfare has always done – the losers of the energy transition away from fossil fuels; second, to get citizens to accept making sacrifices by sharing the costs via progressive taxes; and, third, to forge the national resilience that is necessary to defend democracy from the consequences of climate change, including the outbreak of other pandemics.[5]

163

Yet welfarism has done little to strengthen bonds of reciprocity, as means testing is often humiliating and the benefits system imposes a 'culture of compliance' over 'a culture of trust'.

But the nation as the body politic is essential because it acts as a mediating force between the global and the local – like a vital organ in relation to the arteries. The nation and the specific form of statehood in which a nation is embodied are more able to command popular consent and drive both institutional and cultural change than any system of global governance, never mind a world government – as Lieven rightly reminds us. The pandemic reveals the importance of an activist state and targeted government intervention in dealing with a viral emergency. The same applies analogously to climate change. Western states and emerging powers elsewhere should adopt a range of policies that are not limited to fighting climate change based on lower carbon emissions but also extend to reversing the loss of biodiversity.

One area of focus should be rewilding linked to nature-friendly farming. In response to the failure of global capitalism and the looming ecological disaster, 'a contemporary agrarian movement has arisen which has a lot in common with the agrarian populist and neo-populist movements of a century ago, empha-sising self-reliant, low impact, low energy, land-based lifestyles, a fair distribution of resources, greater political autonomy and so on'.[6] To support this nascent rural revolution, a rebalancing is needed away from large-scale high-tech farming focused on maximum profits towards low-input organic farming with a range of small- and medium-sized farms that supply the local, regional and national economy. The goal is a more resilient and sustainable agriculture built on small farms, market gardens, dairies and forestry businesses that can offer fresh local, seasonal produce. Combined with changes to land ownership and land taxation as proposed by figures such as Henry George,[7] this would over time replace large landholdings reliant on exploited casual labour with many more smallholders who till their land by employing a large workforce – a contribution to job creation in the wake of mass unemployment caused by Covid-19.

A renewal of more sustainable farming would require not just the breakup of agro-industrial conglomerates but also the creation of a more plural network of distribution and small-scale food processing: more small butchers and charcutiers, more vintners and micro-brewers as well as more local bakers and cake makers instead of a plutocracy of six mega supermarket chains that control distribution and can exercise monopsony power.[8] More economically sustainable farming will have ecological benefits and also help to make countries more resilient to shocks while rebuilding depressed economies, especially in rural and coastal areas.

And besides tackling the underlying economic conditions, a postliberal farming policy would also have to focus on habitat protection and restoration. Going forward, farm subsidies should be tied to habitat restoration together with support for the revival of farm wildlife. Agriculture needs to be linked to afforestation, land improvement for wildlife and water conservation as well as rewilding. The writer and conservationist Ruth Davis has argued that,

> At its best, rewilding offers a vision of a more varied, less manicured land, in which natural processes and our imaginations roam free. It has been the driving force behind fantastic projects like Knepp; it has

165

enabled the return of lost species; and has inspired many young people who long for a deeper connection with nature. Using weather, water and native species to help rebuild the complexity of large landscapes also underpins many other fabulous restoration projects, from the massive Cairngorms Connect to coastal wetland recreation at Wallasea on England's east coast.[9]

While acknowledging that rewilding can be seen to be anti-farming and anti-house building, Davis proposes a ten-point biodiversity plan – in response to the Johnson government's ten-point climate plan. The policies she puts forward are as radical as they are traditional, renewing in imaginative ways the legacy of conservation movements. They include: (1) habitation restoration, notably the regeneration and replanting of native forests to capture carbon; (2) protecting rivers and lakes, in particular river 're-wiggling' (i.e. allowing rivers and drainage ditches to provide space for wildlife by letting nature take its own course), financed by a levy on water companies; (3) protecting the coasts by creating a 'mile-deep nature regeneration zone inland from the coastal path, with grants to restore habitats and introduce nature-friendly farming';[10] (4) community-led marine reserves, protecting precious wildlife areas and granting preferential access to local sustainable fishing companies; and (5) rebuilding twentieth-century garden cities as nature cities, with an emphasis on beauty, access to allotments for growing food and proper-sized local parks. All this is part of a wider focus on the connections between natural conservation and urban planning, linked to wildlife regeneration through rebirding and forms of farming that fuse ecology with the restoration of landscape alive with nature.[11]

National Civic Service

This brings us back to the idea of a National Nature Service that would create work and organize people around their attachment to land and labour. Yet individual initiatives such as the NNS often fail on account of insufficient political or institutional support. They either fail to gain traction with decision-makers or are piecemeal projects that lack scope and ambition – like David Cameron's National Citizen Service. The NNS is a bold idea that needs a wider ecosystem of institutions. It should be created as part of an overarching vision of a National Civic Service with potentially three strands: natural, civilian and emergency service. Besides the natural service as just outlined, the recovery from forty years of liberal economics will also require a new civilian service: people, especially the young and the old, either building or using their skills to make a contribution to society. This could take the form of helping elderly people at home, in hospitals or in care homes, mentoring children in schools or extra-curricular activities and helping new residents integrate into the communities by teaching them English and civic education. For the young who are unemployed, this will provide paid work, equipping them with new skills but also vital life experience and the nurturing of a sense of civic obligations, while older, retired people would continue to make a contribution to their community and country: education, childcare, looking after our cultural inheritance and helping with the stewardship of nature.

The emergency service strand would help build up more capacity for national resilience in addition to military capability. At a time when national security expands to include not just food, water and energy but also transportation and the manufacturing of key medical and other supplies, the UK and the US would benefit from a new generation of volunteers who would help with immediate relief in response to natural disasters such as storms, flooding and wildfires, as well as irrigation for areas hit by droughts or the emergency repair of coastal areas affected by erosion. With the armed forces facing new threats such as cyber insecurity, it is vital for states to upgrade the full range of their civilian capabilities. A comprehensive National Civic Service with separate Nature, Society and Emergency strands would complement the policies outlined in the previous chapter on building a new social covenant. It would also go some way towards filling the void at the heart of the West's hollowed-out statecraft and taking more concrete action on climate change.

14

Promoting civic internationalism

Is civilization the new pivot of geopolitics? Brexit, Trump and the resurgence of Russia, China, India and Turkey have put culture and civilizational development at the heart of both domestic politics and foreign policy. From the 'culture wars', which are sweeping the West, to the pushback against Western universalism in much of the non-Western world, civilizational norms appear to be as important as military might or economic prosperity. After decades of Western triumphalism, the supposedly universal values of liberalism are not only contested but also seen by many powers around the globe as subordinate to national cultures or civilizational traditions. As Christopher Coker puts it in his book *The Rise of the Civilizational State*, we are 'living in a world in which civilization is fast becoming the currency of international politics'.[1]

Civilizational states vs nation-states

To say this is not to subscribe to the 'clash of civilizations' thesis based on some form of cultural determinism about inevitable conflicts between fixed civilizational

169

blocks.[2] Instead, the argument is that the new fault lines both inside and across countries are people's cultural identities: how does globalization affect plural ways of life, and how can nations cooperate with one another while also preserving their distinctive cultures? Whereas the Cold War involved a competition between two rival ideologies within the wider Western civilization, the emerging era of international politics is a contest over different civilizational standards in the face of threats to our common humanity from the forces of capitalism, nationalism and technology. The fight America and China are engaged in is not primarily about whether market fundamentalism or state capitalism is the superior ideological model but rather about which culture can shape a politics of society capable of combining consent at home with appeal abroad. The Covid-19 pandemic has intensified this dynamic. Following the storming of the Capitol by Trump supporters on 6 January 2021, Hua Chunying, a spokeswoman for the Chinese foreign ministry, declared that Americans might 'pride themselves on their democracy and freedom', but after witnessing so much political chaos, 'deep down they may hope they could lead a life as the Chinese do'.[3]

For two centuries, the hegemony of the West was linked to its promotion of liberal ideas. Now that liberalism is in crisis, so too is Western influence. The liberalism that has been dominant for the past forty years or so focused on individual freedom and opportunity, which often amounts to free choice or the promotion of global mobility and endless change. But over time, this clashes with people's sense of belonging and their search for settled ways of life – around home, community and country. Populism and authoritarianism tap into a wellspring of anxieties and legitimate grievances to which the mainstream parties and Western powers have had no compelling answer. As the West's political power and moral authority wane, the liberal world order and liberal democracy are in retreat.[4]

The West is deeply divided over what it stands for and how to respond to new threats: from climate change, tech platforms or viral emergencies to the rise of non-Western powers. Meanwhile, the centre of global geopolitics is shifting from the Atlantic to the Eurasian plain and the Asia-Pacific rimland. As the historian John Darwin argued in his book *After Tamerlane*, 'the centre of gravity in modern history lies in Eurasia – in the troubled, conflicted, connected and intimate relations of its great cultures and states, strung out in a line from the European 'Far West' to the Asian 'Far East".[5] The rising challengers of Eurasia have embraced the model of the civilizational state – a state not defined primarily in ethnic, national or territorial terms but rather as the embodiment of a unique civilization. The rise of civilizational states is not just changing the global balance of power. It is also transforming geopolitics away from liberal universalism towards cultural exceptionalism as we enter what many call a post-American, post-Western world.[6]

Chinese leader Xi Jinping champions a model of 'socialism with Chinese characteristics', fusing a Leninist state with neo-Confucian culture. Vladimir Putin defines Russia as a 'state-civilization', which is neither Western nor Asian but uniquely Eurasian. Populist leaders seek to rescue Western civilization from what they see as the ills of multiculturalism and mass immigration. Common to these leaders is a hybrid doctrine of nationalism at home and the defence of civilization abroad. It reconciles their promotion of great-power status with their ideological aversion to liberal universalism.[7] States based on civilizational

171

identities are bound to collide with the institutions of the liberal world order. Emmanuel Macron is one of the few Western leaders to acknowledge the nature and depth of the current crisis: 'We see that we have a crisis with the multilateral framework of 1945: a crisis in terms of its effectiveness, but, and it is even more serious in my opinion, a crisis in terms of the universality of the values upheld by its structures.'[8]

The liberal West and the civilizational states of China and Russia are locked in a battle over competing 'civilizing' missions. And meaningful dialogue between civilizations is becoming more difficult just when mutual understanding is more necessary than ever. The terms of debate between different civilizations are unlikely to be Western. As Coker argues, the pushback by the non-Western world means that 'the West may be out of the business of shaping history for everyone else or even itself'.[9] One plausible scenario is that the decisive conflicts of the future will not be between the West and Asia but among oligarchic and demagogic forces on each side. The world is sliding into a soft totalitarianism based on surveillance and social control. Now that liberal universalism is in crisis, a new global 'culture war' is pitting conservative nationalists against liberal cosmopolitans. Macron recognizes the new shape of international politics:

> Elements such as the dignity of the human person, which were inviolable, and to which all the peoples of the United Nations, all the countries represented, fundamentally subscribed, are now being challenged, played down. There is a perspective emerging today, which is really a break, and which is the game of powers that are not comfortable with the United Nations' human rights framework. There is very clearly a Chinese game, a Russian game on this matter, which promotes playing down values and principles.[10]

172

Values aligned to interests

The populist insurgency and the rise of civilizational states are part of the same phenomena: a backlash against a politics of the global rather than the national and the local; a politics of utopia rather than place; and a politics of individualized identity rather than shared belonging. After decades of accelerating globalization, the world is witnessing a slowdown and even a reversal. Deglobalization, protectionism and border control coincide with a resurgence of nationalism and even atavistic ethnocentrism. All this is very dangerous, but by the same token opens up a space in which politics and the economy can be restructured. Instead of binaries such as globalism versus nativism, the task is to rethink the local together with the national and the international and to do so around shared interests with a moral purpose: the dignity of human labour, the sacred character of our common home of nature and people's belonging to places. Such an approach avoids a binary choice between cynical pragmatism and abstract idealism in favour of ethical realism.

An ethically realist strategy can hold in balance particular interests and universal justice. This paradox was somewhat articulated by Lord Palmerston, who as foreign secretary declared in a speech in the House of Commons on 1 March 1848:

> I hold that the real policy of England – apart from questions which involve her own particular interests, political or commercial – is to be the champion of justice and right; pursuing that course with moderation and prudence […] in pursuing that course, and in pursuing the more limited direction of our own particular interests, my conviction is [… England] never

will find herself altogether alone. [...] We have no eternal allies and we have no perpetual enemies. Our interests are eternal and perpetual, and those interests it is our duty to follow.[11]

Keeping in line with paradox, the old is the new, and a more ethical foreign policy has to be shaped by the pursuit of interests. Yet faced with an increasingly fragmented and polycentric world, Britain and the 'rest of the West' cannot uphold their own best traditions by being divided along national or nation-state lines. Here we return to an earlier argument about the nature of pluralism and corporatism. Just as democratic corporatism cannot flourish when it is too dependent on the executive, it also cannot survive in international isolation. If a plural and democratic corporatism between estranged interests can be negotiated at the national level, then new forms of confederal cooperation across borders are equally possible. International organizations from the UN via NATO to the International Labour Organization (ILO) and the World Health Organization (WHO) or cooperative arrangements between trade unions or faith communities all demonstrate this in different ways.

And if relationships and institutions are more primary than formal treaties, then the nation-state is embedded in the social, cultural ties between peoples and nations and not absolutely sovereign because it does not represent society. By contrast, internationally mingled sovereignty is more democratic if combined with an internally pluralistic devolution of power and resources. Pooling national sovereignty upwards can subject global economic operations to some measure of political control. Democratic nations need to nurture a new international civic covenant, a partnership that is built on people, places and a sense of belonging.

174

Internationalism reinvented

Here we can see the importance of distinguishing peoples and nations from forms of statehood. Whereas states are – perhaps inevitably – exceptionalist, a vast majority of people value their own ordinariness. George Orwell called it the 'unofficial life' – and it is in a belief in one another and local places that love of one's country often expresses itself. Most people do not attach to this sentiment labels like patriotism, nor do they glorify nationalism. Rather, they have deep bonds of affections and attachment to the land and to fellow citizens, which is more instinctive than rational. As Robert Colls writes, 'Patriotism as most British people understand it is more like the old street football than belief in an ideology of some kind – something local and near to hand, open but partisan, unwritten but under-stood, conventional but inventive at the same time, ever-shifting but always the same.'[12]

The alternative to a fragmented globalization is neither nationalism nor failed multilateralism but a civic internationalism of cooperative states anchored in strong institutions that devolve power to people and distribute wealth among social classes and generations. We need new forms of international cooperation to channel capital into productive activities and uphold workers' rights and environmental standards. One way is to empower institutions such as the ILO and strengthen ties between free, democratic trade unions, as Maurice Glasman has suggested.[13] Another way is to build cross-border public green investment banks, agricultural cooperatives and distribution networks for small and medium-sized enterprise. More R&D investment to increase domestic production of critical medical supplies should go hand in hand with greater international collaboration and solidarity: the Pfizer and BioNTech Covid-19 vaccine was developed by a German–Turkish couple, funded by an American pharmaceutical company, manufactured in Belgium and first authorized in the UK. Such cross-border cooperation will prove vital against the existential threats that haunt this century.

As America's political appeal is waning and its moral authority has already collapsed, the West faces a dire destiny of division and irrelevance. With the EU split along multiple lines yet stubbornly avoiding disintegration (including the eurozone), who can promote civic internationalism? For mid-sized powers like the UK, whose economy is the fifth largest in the world but represents only 2 per cent of global GDP, this has profound implications. After Brexit and Covid, its place in the world is radically different to what it was in the 1990s or the 2000s. Out of the EU and with multilateralism on the backfoot, the UK will likely rely more on bilateral ties with allies old and new. As globalization fragments, national economic development will be a key task. International politics looks set to be dominated by America and China, with the EU and Russia desperately trying to gain some strategic autonomy vis-à-vis the two global superpowers, although currently they are sucked into either a US- or a Sino-centric orbit.

Britain's place in the world

Faced with the spectre of Scottish independence and a reunified island of Ireland, the breakup of the Union would further weaken England and Wales internationally. On the one hand, Britain's weakness is likely to reduce it to the status of rule-taker rather than leading rule-maker – especially vis-à-vis the US, China but also the EU. With weak state capacity, a hollowed-out military decimated by ten years of austerity (not reversed by the Johnson government's £24 bn defence spending splurge) and a lack of leadership, how can the UK exercise leverage to build a new international alliance anchored in democratic politics and in the dignity of the person? On the other hand, there are common interests shared between nations that Britain could pursue to bring democracy and place back into its relationship with the world.

Part of that strategy is to recognize that in the long run and after the end of the Putin presidency the UK could take a lead in bringing Russia and its European neighbours – notably Ukraine, Belarus and Poland, but also Scandinavia – into a new Northern European trade and security partnership. The alternative is perpetual confrontation with Russia and its humili-ation of becoming a vassal state to China. To escape the downward spiral in which East–West relations are caught, London could work with Paris and Berlin to bring Moscow in from the cold and into new treaty arrangements akin to the Helsinki process of 1973–5, brokered by the Vatican, that helped to bring the Cold War to a peaceful end. De-escalation and reconciliation with Russia would rebalance relations across Europe and with North America – even if such a course of action takes decades.

And as Glasman has argued, Britain could also build a coalition of islands that are threatened by rising sea levels and fears of continental domination.[14] Hong Kong, Taiwan and Japan are islands threatened by the spectre of Chinese hegemony and ecological devastation. New Zealand, the West Indies and Sri Lanka are island

177

archipelagos with links to the wider Commonwealth, which at its best is a civic covenant and trading association built around the paradoxical combination of ancient liberties with modern democracy. Britain's inheritance is a resource to shape the emerging international order.

One of the UK's greatest assets is its bilateral relationship with France. The lynchpin of post-1945 European security has depended on the military alliance of the UK and France, and, post-Brexit, this bilateral relationship will only become more important – whether in relation to the UN Security Council members, or as the only two nuclear powers in Europe, or their combined task force on cross-channel migration, or their shared maritime border, or their colonial legacies. While Germany and France are united on many EU issues, their ties do not have as yet the historical, cultural or political breadth and depth of Franco-British ties – however conflictual in history. The question is: what direction should that established alliance take in terms of Germany, the US and Russia?

Britain, despite decades of self-mutilation, still has considerable military might and recognized scientific and technical expertise. The UK has to rebuild its armed forces. It is not fantastical to suggest that a strengthened navy could project some power as far as the Gulf and even beyond – especially if Britain intensifies its cooperation with France and helps to shape a less US-dominated NATO. Meanwhile, UK leadership in the search for a Covid-19 vaccine shows that British science is still powerful. The discovery of the vaccine was the combined result of government bringing together academic research and business capacity and using taxpayers' money to establish a new key industry in Britain. We need to become still more a source of expertise and knowledge in high tech and telecommunications to compete with China, but also the arts and humanities. That means a radical rebuilding of research infrastructure, starting with a tripartite system of academic institutions, hybrid institutions that are part-academic and part-vocational (for subjects such as medicine, law, engineering, banking and finance) and vocational/technical colleges for manual work. Above all it requires a reversal of declining standards in many subjects, especially in the humanities.

For Britain to exercise leverage and leadership, it has to link military expansion to the expansion of expertise. The UK should aspire to be the source of all sorts of reliable task forces to tackle pressing problems, such as vaccination, flood defences or irrigation systems, but also strengthening civic institutions like the BBC and building charter cities and free ports together with the countries of the former Hanseatic League. If UK practices reach a quality that other countries will copy, then Britain can lead both by example and by organization.

One way is to enhance cooperation both with Francophonia and with the Commonwealth countries. If new alliances of nations are to be forged, then they have to be more than trading ties in order to be effective. There needs to be some sort of shared politico-economic agenda, besides a military dimension. This involves working towards a new consensus about treatment of labour, fiscal policies to a degree and environmental ones, agreements for policies of mutual protection in trade (instead of either free trade or unilateral protectionism) – even though that can only come gradually – as well as intellectual property. New alliances need to be linked to fair trade and fair treatment of labour. But maybe that could be approached more positively rather than punitively, for example by giving degrees of preferential treatment to those countries and corpora-tions whose practices are relatively good. Peoples and nations will want to be linked to something one can trust and so one can be more competitive by being more ethical.

Britain is currently diminished by internal divisions over Brexit and the handling of the Covid-19 pandemic, but it remains a country of immense skill and forbearance. This could be its last chance to build on its inherent advantages of character before technocratic liberalism or demagogic populism finally erodes them. The UK can only recover a position of influence needed to shape an emerging civic internationalism if it initially regains respect for the British way of doing things at home: a radical, eccentric pragmatism based on humility, hard work and humour.

Renewing the West

Beyond Britain, the West as a political community is in retreat from the international arena. By becoming synonymous with being a liberal civilization, the Western alliance has produced great material achievements that weaken the cultural resources on which the West's identity depends – most of all cooperation and trust in institutions. Wealth without a concern for the common good and power without a shared ethical purpose induce complacency, boredom, decadence and a lack of resolve to deal with decline.[15] At present, Western powers look ill prepared for national and international renewal. Bereft of belief in its own noble traditions, the West has abandoned a generous outlook and, despite Biden's best intentions, fails to lead by example.

The growing backlash against globalization is ampli-fying the call to retreat to narrow national self-interest.

As the boundaries between legitimate wealth and crime are becoming blurred, the world now looks set to slide into corruption, criminality and a disregard for the rule of law from which the West is by no means exempt. To retreat to an insular powerlessness in the face of these threats would be to betray the best traditions of Western civilization and threaten long-term security and flourishing. The only alternative to both chauvinist nationalism and abstract cosmopolitanism is to re-envision the West as something like a commonwealth of nations that reflects a relational covenant among peoples where substantive social and cultural ties based on a common heritage shape our sense of belonging more than trade or formal treaties.

Once more it is Macron who conceptualizes this perhaps more clearly than any other Western leader at present:

> I think it is vital that our Europe finds the ways and means to decide for itself, to rely on itself, not to depend on others, in every area, technological, [...] but also health, geopolitics, and to be able to cooperate with whomever it chooses. Why? Because I think that we are a cohesive geographical space in terms of values, in terms of interests, and that it is good to defend it, in itself. We are an aggregation of different peoples and different cultures. There is no such concentration of so many languages, cultures and diversity in any given geographical space. But something unites us. We know that we are European when we are outside of Europe. We feel our differences when we are among Europeans, but we feel nostalgia when we leave Europe.[16]

Interestingly, this echoes Edmund Burke's conception of Europe as a cultural commonwealth: a polity of nations and peoples who have civilizational norms in common.[17] Macron's Burkean vision of Europe as a continent of shared values and a sense of belonging is not only fundamentally different from a federal super-state but also constitutes a promising basis for a strong partnership with Britain post-Brexit. And emphasizing Europe's distinctive economic model, its belief in the value of high culture and its social-cultural ties with Russia and the Middle East, he states unambiguously that 'we are not the United States of America'. This opens up a geopolitical space in which Europe can have political and strategic autonomy vis-à-vis Washington and provide an alternative to prevent what Macron calls the 'Chinese–American duopoly'.

This conception of Europe has the potential to strengthen the West as it tries to confront both internal and external challenges: Islamism, far-right authori-tarianism, Xi Jinping's totalitarian temptations as well as the task of forging a Euro-African alliance. The many shared traditions that bind together Western cultures across geographical and linguistic boundaries include the Roman idea of citizenship, the Greek notion of a free city, Germanic common law, Jewish and Christian ethics (the dignity of the person, the virtue of free association and the distinction of religious from political authority) and cultural heritages such as Renaissance humanism, the Enlightenment, classicism and Romanticism. In addition, there are collective memories that characterize the Greater West, above all the shared sacrifice of the two world wars, the fall of the Iron Curtain and, more recently, the trauma of Islamist terrorist attacks. All this provides a common horizon and suggests a shared destiny.

Renewed Western leadership requires a clear set of objectives and the art of establishing priorities. The first priority is to continue fighting ISIS and radical Islamism, which is the single greatest threat to the security of the West – as recent attacks on French teachers and Catholic worshippers show. The second priority is to avoid war between the Atlantic West and Russia as well as between US-backed Israel and Saudi Arabia, on the one hand, and Russia-backed Iran and its Shia allies, on the other hand. That has to involve recognizing the legacy of civilizational interactions between Rome, Persia and Byzantium, combined with reconciling estranged interests in the Middle East and Eurasia – as indicated by Israel's recent peace treaties with the United Arab Emirates and Bahrain, which are officially called 'the Abraham Accords Peace Agreement'.

And the third priority is to transform the international system in a manner that fosters the integration of China and the 'rising rest' while avoiding the danger of a 'Thucydidean Trap': a situation in which a conservative status-quo power (the US) confronts a rising new one (China and possibly India).[18] Such a situation could precipitate hostilities in a context where each side lacks a proper cultural understanding of the other, and neither has a coherent strategy to avert war.

But if we are about to move into a period of severe recession or even depression, then we may face a situation more like that of the 1930s, in which more lurid and extreme ideologies will exert mass appeal. Often these will involve a hybrid mix of emotive nationalism with rationalist futurism, and it will be the large states such as China, Russia and perhaps the US under another Trump-like figure who will be most capable of rendering these hybrids globally dominant.

Faced with this prospect, the UK in alliance with France, Germany and other European partners possesses a unique capacity both for resistance and for crafting an alternative model. At its core lies the search for an internationally just order respectful of persons, of relations, of localities, nations and inherited traditions – in essence, a quest for the acceptable co-belonging of human beings within and alongside the rest of the natural world. Muddling through, which has been the West's default mode since the 1970s, is no guarantee of survival. Like the liberal order, the Western alliance will enter its twilight and mutate into a zombie order unless it renews its own best legacy of seeking to uphold the dignity of the person.

Epilogue: a new battleground of ideas

The interregnum remains unresolved. No ideology has replaced the liberal order that is in question following the Iraq invasion, the financial crisis, Brexit and the election of Trump. Populists of different stripes have challenged the establishment but failed to address the grievances that brought them to power. Authoritarian systems in China and elsewhere are in the ascendancy, yet their totalitarian tendencies will erode popular support and the foundations of oligarchic power. Whether Joe Biden can restore America's authority while at the same time disarming populism and containing authoritarianism is far from certain. Emmanuel Macron and the eventual successor to Angela Merkel will face similar challenges. Both the centre-left and the centre-right struggle to define a politics that can resist not only the pull of centrist technocracy but also the push from either the revolutionary left or the radical right. In a world of political parties dominated by sectional interests and vocal minorities, who speaks for the interests and values of the majority? Who defends the dignity of the person and promotes a politics of society built around the common good?

Epilogue

A new consensus

With the old order dead and the new one yet to be born, in the interregnum – the period between the previous and the next settlement – 'all kinds of morbid symptoms pertain' and 'there is a fraternisation of opposites'.[1] As variants of liberalism and authoritarianism converge and even collude, a space is opening up for genuine, constructive alternatives. Covid-19 has revealed the deep desire for community but also the enduring influence of capitalism, nationalism, scientism and big tech. A politics based on a protective state, mutual markets and civic institutions can shape a new consensus that upholds the dignity of work, supports the family, nurtures community and fosters the cooperation of peoples and nations.

Building a new consensus requires more than a political and policy programme. It has to be anchored in a public philosophy to outflank both technocracy and ideological extremes. A public philosophy expresses the shared ends of political action: serving the common good that encompasses personal fulfilment, convivial societies and a flourishing biosphere. The common good is what binds us together, reconciling estranged interests founded upon mutual constraints. Central to a postliberal philosophy is the exercise of social virtues such as courageous leadership, generous compassion or loyalty to all the generations, the fulfilment of our obligations to others, the defence of pluralism against the domination of any one part of society or the economy, a commitment to the importance of place and a sense of limits on both human and technological power. This is the new battleground of ideas for political parties that seek to offer a transformative politics.

Postliberal policy ideas reflect these organizing principles. Good leadership means the restoration of political judgement over technocracy and demagogy, a proper balance of the three branches of government and a careful nurturing of civil service ethos and excellence. It involves building a more relational economy around the everyday economic experience of people by valuing work (linked to a universal Jobs Guarantee), paying a new 'family wage' and strengthening workers' participation through reformed trade unions and workers' representatives on company boards. Regional and sectoral banks are required to channel capital into the neglected parts of the economy, while a National Development Bank is needed to finance large-scale projects. A democratic corporatism involves recognizing 'key workers' by establishing new training colleges for service sectors, offering better vocational, technical and through-life training and by building workplace democracy with employees on company boards as well as workers self-organizing as part of mutuals within the public sector.

To reweave the social fabric requires support for the family by reflecting caring responsibilities in the tax system and providing more generous parental leave and childcare, recognizing that raising children is work that contributes to society. Helping families demands a proper adult social care system based on mutual insurance – linked to radical reforms of the welfare state that enable people to participate in budgeting and co-designing services. And if we want to care for our common home of nature, we could set up a National Nature Service that puts the protection and restoration of biodiversity first while also acknowledging the centrality of the protective state in fighting climate change. At the same time, a postliberal policy programme involves a new civic internationalism to combat the insurgent nationalist right by forging novel forms of cooperation between nations and peoples – through democratic associations such as trade unions, universities and faith communities. Building a better international order will also require the renewal of the West and its inheritance of personalism, forging a politics and economics of the common good.

A new coalition

We have been here before. Alternatives emerge, but 'third-way' politics ends up getting absorbed into dominant ideologies rather than displacing them. In the 1940s, the personalism of Emmanuel Mounier sought to chart an alternative to both communism and fascism, but Mounier briefly served Vichy, which was an authoritarian client state of Nazi Germany. In the 1990s, Tony Blair – influenced in part by communitarian thinking and the Christian socialism of John Macmurray – promised a 'third way' beyond neoliberalism and statism but ended up promoting liberal globalization. Going forward, how can postliberalism avoid the same fate of failing to transform the status quo?

The new consensus will take time to form and it needs to be sustained with roots in the everyday life of people. Covid-19 reminds us of what really matters: the love for family and friends, the relationships that bind us together as neighbours, colleagues or citizens. Where the dominant ideologies polarize, postliberalism can build new coalitions across class and culture based on common concerns of decent work, support for families, affordable housing, health and social care, good schools and a respect for settled ways of life.

Some of the building blocks for the new coalition are developed in a recent book entitled *Lessons Learned* by the veteran community organizer Arnie Graf.[2] According to him, the four principles for a renewed democratic politics are, first of all, the reality and importance of power. Power is necessary for purposeful change, and through organizing different interests we can create power. But for power to be a force for good, it has to be relational – listening to people, understanding their interests and motivations, as well as building trust and cooperation. Transactional technocracy or ideological fanaticism will lead to prejudice and exclusion. Second, self-interest encompasses not only basic necessities like work, wages to feed yourself and your family, a roof over your head and a safe neighbourhood but also a share in the good life: being recognized for your talents and contribution to society and building relationships with people with whom you agree and disagree.

The third principle is related to Graf's distinction between a problem and an issue. Generally speaking, problems are too big and abstract to be resolved by democratic politics in the short run, but an issue is a particular injustice around which a campaign can be organized and action be coordinated. Whereas a politics focused on problems leads to protest which is often a sign of powerlessness, a politics centred on issues creates collective action – Graf's fourth principle – which leads to a reaction. This, in turn, triggers recognition from political opponents and thereby creates a basis on which to negotiate a compromise. As mentioned in chapter 5, politics as the conciliation of rival interests (Bernard Crick) requires giving each interest a share of power. Since democracies involve both conflict and

Epilogue

compromise, a democratic politics has to acknowledge power and interests but make them the basis for cooperating in pursuit of the common good.

These four principles need to be sustained by an ethos of responsibility, reciprocity and relationships – people forging deep ties of trust and cooperation to create a common life. From local government to civic groups, and from faith communities to ethical enterprise, this ethos is there in abundance and now needs to be harnessed by political representation and popular participation.

A key question therefore is the political form postliberalism might take. So far, no significant political party anywhere across the West has embraced a coherent postliberal vision. Counting on a single leader to convert a party to the cause, as with David Cameron's Big Society or Ed Miliband's One-Nation Labour, has proven to be illusory. Change is likely to come from small, creative minorities who can reflect majority norms and bring with them large organizations through new forms of collaboration. That will require more virtuous and effective leadership combined with greater popular participation – elites leading by example and helping to build deeper democracy. A new economic and social covenant can bring divided communities and nations together: a binding pact that creates a partnership between alienated generations, rival interests and separate regions. Based on institutions that balance rights with obligations and self-interest with mutual benefit, a new covenant binds people into a common life anchored in the public good. Going forward, the new coalition will be built around a politics of society.[3]

At a time when the right is in power in most European countries, the left has to develop a project of national renewal to bridge divisions and rebuild

Epilogue

a cross-class and cross-cultural coalition. Since the deepest divides are around education, age and social class, gaining and retaining power means that the left has to develop a political position which binds together these estranged and even mutual hostile interests and groups in a common cause: a better life centred on the family, community and security (personal, communal and national security all at once). Both Joe Biden and Keir Starmer have done this up to a point by putting working people at the centre of their attempts to renew the centre-left. Refocusing on the things that matter to most people is the best way to regain the trust of lost voters by reflecting the national character and disposition: in the UK, this means being stoic rather than impatient, demoralized yet determined, possessed of calm rather than of rage, imbued with a sense of duty and not a sense of entitlement. It is to build a democratic politics of shared power, rooted in people's everyday experience.[4]

Politics is a struggle for power, and today power is concentrated in the hands of global finance, tech platforms and hostile foreign countries. Peoples and nations need to associate with renewed vigour to create a resilient decentralized democracy which upholds the dignity of labour, the importance of place and our mutual dependence. At present, the future is one of extreme liberalism, demagogic populism and authoritarianism sliding into novel forms of fascism. These spectres from the past have returned to haunt us, and now they demand of the West that it recovers its own best traditions. The task is to build broad coalitions that can win power and shape a new covenant, giving people a share in the things that make life worth living.

Notes

Preface

1 Deborah Mattinson, *Beyond the Red Wall: Why Labour Lost, How the Conservatives Won and What Will Happen Next?* (London: Biteback Publishing, 2020).
2 Adrian Pabst, 'Power without purpose: how the Tories don't have a national plan', *New Statesman*, 14–20 February 2020, pp. 25–7.
3 Michael Lind, *The New Class War: Saving Democracy from the Metropolitan Elite* (London: Atlantic, 2020).

Prologue: a new era

1 Anne Case and Angus Deaton, *Deaths of Despair and the Future of Capitalism* (Princeton, NJ: Princeton University Press, 2020).
2 Lind, *The New Class War*.
3 Weiwei Zhang, *The China Wave: Rise of a Civilizational State* (Shanghai: WCPC, 2012).
4 John Gray, *Postliberalism: Studies in Political Thought* (London: Routledge, 1993); David Goodhart, 'A postliberal future?', *Demos Quarterly*, 1/1 (2014), https://www.demos.co.uk/files/apostliberalfuture.pdf; John Milbank and Adrian Pabst, *The Politics of Virtue: Postliberalism and the Human Future* (London: Rowman

192

& Littlefield International, 2016); cf. Giles Fraser, 'A post-liberal reading list', *UnHerd*, 22 November 2019, https://unherd.com/2019/11/a-post-liberal-reading-list/.

5 Paul Collier and John Kay, *Greed Is Dead: Politics After Individualism* (London: Allen Lane, 2020); Patrick Porter, *The False Promise of Liberal Order: Nostalgia, Delusion and the Rise of Trump* (Cambridge: Polity, 2020).

6 Fred Dallmayr, *Postliberalism: Discovering a Shared World* (Oxford: Oxford University Press, 2019).

7 Raghuram Rajan, *The Third Pillar: The Revival of Community in a Polarised World* (London: William Collins, 2019).

Part I Postliberal times

1 David Lammy, *Out of the Ashes: Britain after the riots*, rev. ed. (London: Guardian Books, 2012).

2 Jon Cruddas, 'One Nation – caring, earning and belonging', speech given to Civitas think-tank, 14 October 2013, http://www.civitas.org.uk/pdf/earningand belonging.pdf.

3 Martin Kettle, 'Brexit was a revolt against liberalism. We've entered a new political era', *The Guardian*, 16 September 2016, https://www.theguardian.com/comment isfree/2016/sep/15/brexit-liberalism-post-liberal-age.

4 Adrian Pabst, 'Postliberalism: the new centre-ground of British politics', *The Political Quarterly*, 88/3 (2017): 500–9; Nick Timothy, *Remaking One Nation: The Future of Conservatism* (Cambridge: Polity, 2020), pp. 1–28.

5 Sohrab Ahmari, 'Power putsch', *The Spectator*, 4 July 2020, p. 14.

Chapter 1 Resolving the interregnum

1 Antonio Gramsci, 'The Third Notebook (1930)', in *Prison Notebooks*, ed. and tr. Joseph A. Buttigieg (New York: Columbia Press, 1996), Vol. 2, §34, pp. 32–3.

2 Ross Douthat, 'The crisis of the liberal zombie order', *New Statesman*, 20–6 March 2020, https://www.newstatesman.com/science-tech/coronavirus/2020/03/crisis-liberal-zombie-order.
3 Lind, *The New Class War*.
4 See Adrian Pabst, 'The Greater West: the limits of liberal civilization and the renewal of Western statecraft', in Russell Berman and Kiron Skinner (eds), *The Future of Western Civilization* (Palo Alto, CA: Stanford University Press, 2021, forthcoming).
5 Minxin Pei, *China's Crony Capitalism: The Dynamics of Regime Decay* (Cambridge, MA: Harvard University Press, 2016); Andrey Movchan, *Decline, Not Collapse: The Bleak Prospects for Russia's Economy* (Moscow: Carnegie Endowment for International Peace, 2017).
6 Shoshana Zuboff, *The Age of Surveillance Capitalism: The Fight for a Human Future at the New Frontier of Power* (London: Profile Books, 2019); Noreena Hertz, *The Lonely Century: Coming Together in a World That's Pulling Apart* (London: Sceptre, 2020).
7 Michael J. Sandel, *The Tyranny of Merit: What's Become of the Common Good?* (New York: Farrar, Straus and Giroux, 2020); David Goodhart, *Head, Hand, Heart: The Struggle for Dignity and Status in the 21*st *Century* (London: Penguin, 2020).
8 Jason Cowley, 'Editor's note', *The New Statesman*, 17 June 2020, https://www.newstatesman.com/politics/uk/2020/06/boris-johnson-stokes-flames-culture-wars-because-he-knows-he-trapped.
9 For an earlier, extended account, see John Milbank and Adrian Pabst, *The Politics of Virtue: Postliberalism and the Human Future* (London: Rowman & Littlefield International, 2016).
10 Patrick Deneen, *Why Liberalism Failed* (New Haven, CT: Yale University Press, 2018), p. 3.
11 Martin Sandbu, *The Economics of Belonging: A Radical Plan to Win Back the Left Behind and Achieve Prosperity for All* (Princeton, NJ: Princeton University Press, 2020);

Ian Dunt, *How to Be a Liberal: The Story of Liberalism and the Fight for Its Life* (London: Canbury Press, 2020).

12 Timothy Garton Ash, 'The future of liberalism', *Prospect*, January/February 2021, pp. 18–28, https://www.prospectmagazine.co.uk/magazine/the-future-of-liberalism-brexit-trump-philosophy.

13 Sandel, *The Tyranny of Merit*, p. 212.

14 Jonathan Rutherford, 'No wealth but life: the conservative origins of English socialism', *New Statesman*, 22 July 2020, https://www.newstatesman.com/politics/economy/2020/07/no-wealth-life-conservative-origins-english-socialism.

Chapter 2 Politics after the plague

1 Albert Camus, *The Plague*, tr. Robin Buss (London: Penguin, 2001), p. 129.

2 Maurice Glasman, 'As globalisation fractures, the West must champion internationalism in the face of China', *New Statesman*, 3 July 2020, https://www.newstatesman.com/world/asia/2020/07/globalisation-fractures-west-must-champion-internationalism-face-china.

3 Camus, *The Plague*, p. 31.

4 Ibid., p. 125.

5 Ibid.

6 Ibid., p. 33.

7 Edward Docx, 'The peak: inside the mind of Dr Jim Down, a leading intensive care consultant, on the night of the peak number of deaths from Covid-19 in hospitals', *New Statesman*, 27 May 2020, https://www.newstatesman.com/politics/health/2020/05/peak.

8 Maurice Glasman, 'The coronavirus crisis has sounded the death knell for liberal globalisation', *New Statesman*, 12 April 2020, https://www.newstatesman.com/politics/economy/2020/04/coronavirus-crisis-has-sounded-death-knell-liberal-globalisation.

9 Jon Cruddas, *The Dignity of Labour* (Cambridge: Polity, 2021).
10 Sandel, *The Tyranny of Merit*.
11 Ruchir Sharma, *The Rise and Fall of Nations: Forces of Change in the Post-Crisis World* (New York: W.W. Norton & Co., 2016).
12 Karl Marx and Friedrich Engels, *The Manifesto of the Community Party* (1848), https://www.marxists.org/archive/marx/works/1848/communist-manifesto/.
13 Ibid.
14 Matthew Yglesias, 'The Great Awokening', *Vox*, 1 April 2019, https://www.vox.com/2019/3/22/18259865/great-awokening-white-liberals-race-polling-trump-2020.
15 Camus, *The Plague*, p. 195.

Chapter 3 Why opposites coincide

1 Fyodor Dostoevsky, *Demons*, tr. Robert Maguire (London: Penguin, 2008), p. 446. Here I am indebted to conversations with John Gray and Rowan Williams.
2 Helen Pluckrose and James Lindsay, *Cynical Theories: How Universities Made Everything About Race, Gender, and Identity – and Why This Harms Everybody* (London: Allen & Unwin, 2020).
3 Examples include Garton Ash, 'The future of liberalism', and Mark Lilla, *The Once and Future Liberal: After Identity Politics* (New York: HarperCollins, 2017).
4 Ross Douthat, 'The rise of woke capital', *The New York Times*, 28 February 2018, https://www.nytimes.com/2018/02/28/opinion/corporate-america-activism.html; Helen Lewis, 'How capitalism drives cancel culture: beware splashy corporate gestures when they leave existing power structures intact', *The Atlantic*, 14 July 2020, https://www.theatlantic.com/international/archive/2020/07/cancel-culture-and-problem-woke-capitalism/614086/.
5 For contrasting accounts that nonetheless agree on the erosion of Russia's democratic constitution, see Richard

Sakwa, *The Crisis of Russian Democracy: The Dual State, Factionalism and the Medvedev Succession* (Cambridge: Cambridge University Press, 2010); and Mark Galeotti, *We Need to Talk About Putin* (London: Ebury, 2019).

6 Samuel Taylor Coleridge, *On the Constitution of the Church and State According to the Idea of Each* (London: Routledge & Kegan Paul, 1976 [1830]).

7 Joel Kotkin, *The Coming of Neo-Feudalism: A Warning to the Global Middle Class* (New York: Encounter Books, 2020), p. 7.

8 Thomas Piketty, *Capital and Ideology*, tr. Arthur Goldhammer (Cambridge, MA: Harvard University Press, 2020).

9 Claire Ainsley, *The New Working Class: How to Win Hearts, Minds and Votes* (Bristol: Policy Press, 2018).

10 Carl E. Walter and Fraser J.T. Howie, *Red Capitalism: The Fragile Financial Foundation of China's Extraordinary Rise* (Oxford: Wiley, 2011).

11 Peter Pomerantsev, *Nothing Is True and Everything Is Possible: Adventures in Modern Russia* (London: Faber & Faber, 2015).

12 Emily Kenway, *The Truth About Modern Slavery* (London: Pluto Press, 2021); Genevieve LeBaron, *Combatting Modern Slavery: Why Labour Governance is Failing and What We Can Do About It* (Cambridge: Polity, 2020).

13 Aris Roussinos, 'Covid has exposed America as a failed state', *UnHerd*, 1 June 2020, https://unherd.com/2020/06/covid-has-exposed-america-as-a-failed-state/.

14 Richard Sennett, *The Corrosion of Character: The Personal Consequences of Work in the New Capitalism* (New York: W.W. Norton, 1999); *The Culture of New Capitalism* (New Haven: Yale University Press, 2007).

15 Mary Midgley, *Beast and Man: The Roots of Human Nature* (Ithaca, NY: Cornell University Press, 1978).

16 Mary Midgley, *Wisdom, Information and Wonder: What Is Knowledge For?* (London: Routledge, 1989).

17 Zuboff, *The Age of Surveillance Capitalism.*

18 Nathan VanderKlippe, 'Chinese blacklist an early

glimpse of sweeping new social-credit control', *The Globe and Mail*, 3 January 2018, https://www.theglobeandmail.com/news/world/chinese-blacklist-an-early-glimpse-of-sweeping-new-social-credit-control/article37493300/.

Chapter 4 New polarities

1 Marcel Gauchet, 'The right and the left', in Pierre Nora (ed.), *Realms of Memory: Rethinking the French Past, Vol. I: Conflicts and Divisions* (New York: Columbia University Press, 1996), pp. 241–99.
2 Roger Eatwell and Matthew Goodwin, *National Populism: The Revolt Against Liberal Democracy* (London: Penguin, 2018).
3 For rival versions of this thesis, see David Goodhart, *The Road to Somewhere: The New Tribes Shaping British Politics* (London: Penguin, 2017); Pippa Norris and Ronald Inglehart, *Cultural Backlash: Trump, Brexit, and Authoritarian Populism* (Cambridge: Cambridge University Press, 2019).
4 Gladden Pappin, 'From conservatism to postliberalism: the right after 2020', *American Affairs*, IV/3 (Fall 2020), pp. 174–90.
5 Yoram Hazony, *The Virtue of Nationalism* (New York: Basic Books, 2018).
6 Oren M. Cass, *The Once and Future Worker: A Vision for the Renewal of Work in America* (New York: Encounter Books, 2018).
7 Roger Scruton, *How to Be a Conservative* (London: Bloomsbury, 2014); *Conservatism: An Invitation to the Great Tradition* (London: All Points Books, 2017).
8 Christophe Guilluy, *No society: la fin de la classe moyenne occidentale* (Paris: Flammarion, 2018).
9 John Milbank, 'In triplicate: Britain after Brexit; the world after coronavirus; retrospect and prospect', *Telos*, 191 (Summer 2020): 91–114.

Part II A public philosophy of postliberalism

1 Simone Weil, *The Need for Roots*, tr. Arthur Wills (London: Routledge & Kegan Paul, 1952), p. 40.
2 Simone Weil, 'Draft for a Statement of Human Obligations', in *Simone Weil: An Anthology*, ed. Siân Miles (London: Penguin, 2005 [1986]), pp. 229–30.

Chapter 5 The art of politics

1 Glasman, 'As globalisation fractures, the West must champion internationalism in the face of China'.
2 Alain Supiot, *La Gouvernance par les nombres: cours au Collège de France, 2012–2014* (Paris: Fayard, 2015).
3 Don Patinkin, *Money, Interest and Prices: An Integration of Monetary and Value Theory* (Evanston, IL: Row, Peterson & Co., 1956), p. 37.
4 Quoted in Martin McCauley, *Bandits, Gangsters and the Mafia: Russia, the Baltic States and the CIS since 1992* (London: Routledge, 2013), p. 260.
5 Diane Coyle, *GDP: A Brief but Affectionate History* (Princeton, NJ: Princeton University Press, 2015); David Pilling, *The Growth Delusion: The Wealth and Well-Being of Nations* (London: Bloomsbury, 2018).
6 'The Queen's broadcast to the UK and Commonwealth', 5 April 2020, https://www.royal.uk/queens-broadcast-uk-and-commonwealth.
7 Richard H. Thaler and Cass R. Sunstein, *Nudge: Improving Decisions about Health, Wealth, and Happiness* (New Haven, CT: Yale University Press, 2008).
8 William Davies, 'Coronavirus and the rise of rule-breakers', *New Statesman*, 8 July 2020, https://www.newstatesman.com/2020/07/coronavirus-and-rise-rule-breakers.
9 See Milbank and Pabst, *The Politics of Virtue*, pp. 69–90.
10 James Williams, *Stand Out of Our Light: Freedom and Resistance in the Attention Economy* (Cambridge: Cambridge University Press, 2018).
11 John Gray, 'State of the nation: why we are entering a new

age of disorder', *The New Statesman*, 8 July 2020, https:// www.newstatesman.com/politics/uk/2020/07/state-nation.

12 Bernard Crick, *In Defence of Politics*, 4th edn (University of Chicago Press, 1992), p. 24.

13 Ibid., p. 141.

14 Ibid., pp. 18 and 21.

15 Ibid., p. 24.

16 Alasdair MacIntyre, *After Virtue: A Study in Moral Theory*, 3rd edn (London: Duckworth, 2001 [1981]).

17 The first quote is taken from Edmund Burke, 'On a Motion for leave to bring in a Bill to repeal and alter certain Acts respecting Religious Opinions: May 11, 1792', in *The Works of Edmund Burke* (London: Bell, 1906), Vol. III, p. 317, and the second is taken from Edmund Burke, 'Letter to Sir Hercules Langrishe (1782)', in *The Writings and Speeches of Edmund Burke*, Vol. 9, ed. R.B. McDowell and William B. Todd (Oxford: Oxford University Press, 1991), p. 250.

18 Lind, *The New Class War*.

19 Mervyn King and John Kay, *Radical Uncertainty: Decision-Making for an Unknowable Future* (Boston, MA: Little, Brown, 2020).

Chapter 6 Social virtues

1 John Gray, *Isaiah Berlin* (Princeton, NJ: Princeton University Press, 1996), p. 1; cf. Isaiah Berlin, *The Crooked Timber of Humanity: Chapters in the History of Ideas* (New York: Vintage Books, 1992).

2 Jonathan Rutherford, 'The closing of the conservative mind: towards a new left conservatism', *The New Statesman*, 26 June 2019, https://www.newstatesman. com/politics/uk/2019/06/closing-conservative-mind-towards-new-left-conservatism.

3 John Rawls, 'The idea of an overlapping consensus', *Oxford Journal of Legal Studies*, 7/1 (1987): 1–25.

4 MacIntyre, *After Virtue*, pp. 1–42.

5 Edmund Burke, *Reflections on the Revolution in France*

(1790), in Ian Hampsher-Monk (ed.), *Burke: Revolutionary Writings* (Cambridge: Cambridge University Press, 2014), p. 101.

6 Lewis Mumford, *Values for Survival: Essays, Addresses, and Letters on Politics and Education* (New York: Harcourt Brace, 1946), p. 184.

7 Will Tanner, James O'Shaughnessy, Fjolla Krasniqi and James Blagden (eds), *State of Our Social Fabric: Measuring the Changing Nature of Community over Time and Geography* (London: Onward, 2020).

8 Robert D. Putnam and Shaylyn Romney Garrett, *The Upswing: How America Came Together a Century Ago and How We Can Do It Again* (New York: Simon & Schuster, 2020).

9 Lester K. Born, ed. and tr., *The Education of a Christian Prince, by Desiderius Erasmus* (New York: Columbia University Press, 1936), pp. 209 and 233.

10 Cicero, *De Inventione*, II, LIII.

11 MacIntrye, *After Virtue*, p. 211.

12 Midgley, *Wisdom, Information and Wonder*, p. 98.

13 See Adrian Pabst, *Metaphysics: The Creation of Hierarchy* (Grand Rapids, MI: Eerdmans, 2012).

14 Burke, *Reflections on the Revolution in France*, p. 47.

15 Mary Midgley, *The Ethical Primate: Humans, Freedom and Morality* (London: Routledge, 1994), p. 134.

Chapter 7 Mutual obligations

1 Christopher Lasch, *The Revolt of the Elites and the Betrayal of Democracy* (New York: W.W. Norton & Co., 1996); Cf. Christopher Lasch, *The Culture of Narcissism: American Life in An Age of Diminishing Expectations* (New York: W.W. Norton & Co., 1979).

2 José Ortega y Gasset, *The Revolt of the Masses*, tr. Anthony Kerrigan (New York: W.W. Norton & Co., 1985).

3 Lasch, *The Revolt of the Elites*, p. 25.

4 Ibid., p. 27. Arguably, G.K. Chesterton had made these points half a century or so before Lasch, namely

in his books *The Common Man* (New York: Sheed & Ward, 1950) and 'On Certain Modern Writers and the Institution of the Family' (1905), in *Heretics* (London: CreateSpace Independent Publishing Platform, 2016), pp. 60–6.

5 Lasch, *The Revolt of the Elites*, p. 27.

6 Ibid., p. 80.

7 Ibid., p. 44.

8 Edmund Burke, 'A letter to M. Depont' (1789) in *Selected Writings and Speeches*, ed. Peter J. Stanlis (London: Transaction Publishers, 2009), p. 507.

9 Edmund Burke, 'A letter from Mr Burke to a Member of the National Assembly; in answer to some objections to his book on French affairs' (1791), in *Selected Writings and Speeches*, p. 615.

10 Ed West, 'How a 1990s book predicted 2020: Christopher Lasch's *The Revolt of the Elites* detailed how capitalism would radicalise the rich', *Unherd*, 3 July 2020, https://unherd.com/2020/07/the-book-that-predicted-2020/.

11 Lasch, *The Revolt of the Elites*, p. 45.

12 Ibid., p. 47.

13 Pope Francis, Encyclical Letter *Laudato Si'*, 24 May 2015, §123, full text available online: http://w2.vatican.va/content/francesco/en/encyclicals/documents/papa-francesco_20150524_enciclica-laudato-si.html.

14 Norman Dennis, *English Ethical Socialism: Thomas More to R.H. Tawney* (New York: Oxford University Press, 1988).

15 David Miller, *Strangers in Our Midst: The Political Philosophy of Immigration* (Cambridge, MA: Harvard University Press, 2016).

16 John Cartwright, *Internal Evidence; or an Inquiry How Far Truth and the Christian Religion Have Been Consulted by the Author of Thoughts on a Parliamentary Reform* (London: Gale ECCO Print Editions, 2018 [1784]), pp. 58–60.

17 Lasch, *The Revolt of the Elites*, p. 49.

Chapter 8 Pluralism

1 David Marquand, 'Pluralism v populism', *Prospect Magazine* 20 June 1999, https://www.prospectmagazine. co.uk/magazine/pluralismvpopulism.
2 Ibid.
3 As documented in the Xinjiang papers published by *The New York Times*, 16 November 2019, https://www. nytimes.com/interactive/2019/11/16/world/asia/china-xinjiang-documents.html.
4 Ibid.
5 Isaiah Berlin, 'Two concepts of liberty', in *Four Essays on Liberty* (Oxford: Oxford University Press, 1969), pp. 118–72.
6 Besides Rawls, 'The idea of an overlapping consensus', see also his *A Theory of Justice* (Cambridge, MA: Harvard University Press, 1971) and *Political Liberalism* (New York: Columbia University Press, 1993).
7 Paul Hirst, *Associative Democracy: New Forms of Economic and Social Governance* (Cambridge: Polity, 1996); Paul Hirst and Veit-Michael Bader (eds), *Associative Democracy: The Real Third Way* (London: Frank Cass, 2001); Paul Hirst (ed.), *The Pluralist Theory of the State: Selected Writings of G.D.H. Cole, J.N. Figgis and H.J. Laski* (London: Routledge, 1989); cf. David Runciman, *Pluralism and the Personality of the State* (Cambridge: Cambridge University Press, 1997).
8 Paolo Grossi, 'Constitutional lawfulness in the history of modern law', *Italian Journal of Public Law*, 2 (2012), http://www.ijpl.eu/archive/2012/issue-21/constitutional-lawfulness-in-the-history-of-modern-law, p. 274 (original emphasis).
9 Karl Polanyi, *The Great Transformation: The Political and Economic Origins of Our Time* (Boston, MA: Beacon Press, 2001 [1944]).
10 Antonio Genovesi, *Lezioni di commercio o sia di economia civile*, intro. by Luigino Bruni and Stefano Zamagni, ed.

Francesca Dal Degan (Milan: Vita e Pensiero, 2013 [1765–7]), pp. 30–1.

11 Marquand, 'Pluralism v populism'.

12 Lind, *The New Class War*, p. 136.

13 Emmanuel Mounier, *Personalism*, tr. Philip Mairet (Notre Dame, IN: University of Notre Dame Press, 1970 [1950]).

14 Thomas Traherne, 'The third century', in *Selected Writings*, ed. D. Davis (Manchester: Carcanet Press, 1992), p. 93.

15 Benedetto Gui, 'From transactions to encounters: the joint generation of relational goods and conventional values', in Benedetto Gui and Robert Sugden (eds), *Economics and Social Interaction* (Cambridge: Cambridge University Press, 2005), pp. 23–51.

16 On the Axial Age and its crucial legacy for the idea of dignity of the person, see Karl Jaspers, *The Origin and Goal of History*, tr. Michael Bullock (London: Routledge & Kegan Paul, 1953); Robert Bellah, *Religion in Human Evolution: From the Paleolithic to the Axial Age* (Cambridge, MA: Harvard University Press, 2011); Robert Bellah and Hans Joas (eds), *The Axial Age and Its Consequences* (Cambridge, MA: The Belknap Press of Harvard University, 2011).

17 Maurice Glasman, 'The good society, Catholic social thought and the politics of the common good', in Ian Geary and Adrian Pabst (eds), *Blue Labour: Forging a New Politics* (London: I.B. Tauris, 2015), p. 14.

18 Marquand, 'Pluralism v populism'.

Chapter 9 Place, limits and ecology

1 World Wildlife Fund, 'Living Planet Report 2020', https://livingplanet.panda.org/en-us/.

2 Timothy Morton, *Being Ecological* (London: Penguin, 2018).

3 Pope Francis, Encyclical Letter *Laudato Si'*.

4 R.H. Tawney, *The Acquisitive Society* (London: Bell,

1921); see also his seminal book *Religion and the Rise of Capitalism* (New Brunswick, NJ: Transaction, 1998), esp. pp. 79–132.

5 Rowan Williams, 'Embracing our limits: the lessons of *Laudato Si*", *Commonweal*, 23 September 2015, https://www.commonwealmagazine.org/embracing-our-limits.

6 Karl Polanyi, *Primitive, Archaic and Modern Economies: Essays of Karl Polanyi*, ed. George Dalton (New York: Anchor Books, 1968); Marcel Mauss, *The Gift: The Form and Reason for Exchange in Archaic Societies*, tr. W.D. Halls (New York: W.W. Norton, 2000); Jacques T. Godbout and Alain Caillé, *The World of the Gift*, tr. D. Winkler (Montreal: McGill-Queen's University Press, 1998).

7 Weil, *The Need for Roots*.

8 John Milbank, 'Between catastrophes: God, nature and humanity', in Alexander Hampton (ed.), *Pandemic, Ecology and Theology: Perspectives on COVID-19* (London: Routledge, 2020), pp. 78–89 (original emphasis).

9 Lasch, *Revolt of the Elites*, p. 48 (emphasis added). What Lasch calls 'nationalism' is not the right-wing adulation of ethnic homogeneity but rather a broad patriotic commitment to one's country and culture, to place and people.

10 See *Ian Hislop's Age of the Do-Gooders*, BBC Two; Simon Heffer, *High Minds: The Victorians and the Birth of Modern Britain* (London: Random House, 2013).

11 John Tomaney, 'Parochialism – a defence', *Progress in Human Geography*, 37/5 (2012), p. 658.

12 Robert D. Kaplan, *The Revenge Of Geography: What The Map Tells Us About Coming Conflicts and the Battle Against Fate* (New York: Random House, 2012).

13 Tomaney, 'Parochialism – a defence', p. 662.

14 Ibid., p. 663.

15 Roger Scruton, 'Mary Midgley', *Standpoint Magazine*, 5 December 2008, https://standpointmag.co.uk/underrated-january-09/.

Chapter 10 Building a relational economy

1 Paul Collier, *The Future of Capitalism* (London: Penguin, 2019).
2 E.P. Thompson, 'The moral economy of the English crowd in the 18th century', *Past and Present*, 50 (1971): 76–136; and E.P. Thompson, *Customs in Common: Studies in Traditional Popular Culture* (London: Merlin, 1991).
3 Robert D. Atkinson and Michael Lind, 'National developmentalism: from forgotten tradition to new consensus', *American Affairs*, III/2 (Summer 2019): 165–91.
4 Ibid., pp. 179–80.
5 Ibid., p. 190.
6 David Edgerton, *The Rise and Fall of the British Nation: A Twentieth-Century History* (London: Penguin, 2019).
7 Ibid., p. 221.
8 Philip McCann, 'Perceptions of regional inequality and the geography of discontent: insights from the UK', *Regional Studies*, 54/2 (2020): 256–67.
9 Julie Froud, Sukhdev Johal, Michael Moran, Angelo Salento and Karel Williams (on behalf of the Foundational Economy Collective), *Foundational Economy: The Infrastructure of Everyday Life* (Manchester: Manchester University Press, 2018); cf. Rachel Reeves, *The Everyday Economy* (London: Labour Together, 2018).
10 Matt Stoller, *Goliath: The 100-Year War Between Monopoly Power and Democracy* (New York: Simon & Schuster, 2019).
11 See The Final Report of the 2017 Industrial Strategy Commission by Kate Barker, Craig Berry, Diane Coyle, Richard Jones and Andy Westwood, http://industrialstrategycommission.org.uk/wp-content/uploads/2017/10/The-Final-Report-of-the-Industrial-Strategy-Commission.pdf.
12 Brett Christophers, *Rentier Capitalism: Who Owns the Economy, and Who Pays for It?* (London: Verso, 2020).
13 Stacy Mitchell, 'The empire of everything', *The Nation*, 12 March 2018.

14 On the limits of regulating tech platforms and the case for using anti-trust laws, see my *The Demons of Liberal Democracy* (Cambridge: Polity, 2019), pp. 59–65.
15 Elinor Ostrom, *Governing the Commons: The Evolution of Institutions for Collective Action* (Cambridge: Cambridge University Press, 1991).

Chapter 11 Renewing democratic corporatism

1 To acknowledge this does not amount to agreeing with Carl Schmitt on the state of emergency or with Giorgio Agamben's crypto conspiracy that Covid-19, like Sars 2, is little more than a particularly virulent flu bug which caused an excessive reaction designed to suspend all normal procedures in the name of a permanent rule by exception. See Carl Schmitt, *Political Theology: Four Chapters on the Concept of Sovereignty*, trans. George D. Schwab (Cambridge, MA: MIT Press, 1985); Giorgio Agamben, 'The invention of an epidemic', *European Journal of Psychoanalysis*, https://www.journal-psycho analysis.eu/coronavirus-and-philosophers/.
2 Frank Field, 'Rebuilding Beveridge', *Prospect Magazine*, 19 September 2012, https://www.prospectmagazine. co.uk/magazine/rebuilding-beveridge-welfare-frank-field.
3 Collier, *The Future of Capitalism*.
4 Lind, *The New Class War*.
5 Hugh A. Clegg and Allan Flanders (eds), *The System of Industrial Relations in Great Britain: Its History, Law and Institutions* (Oxford: Blackwell, 1954).
6 See James Noyes and Adrian Pabst, 'The only lasting antidote to pandemics is a stronger civil society', *New Statesman*, 29 March 2020, https://www.new statesman.com/politics/economy/2020/03/only-lasting-antidote-pandemics-stronger-civic-society.
7 Groupe d'études géopolitiques, 'The Macron Doctrine: a conversation with the French President', 16 November 2020, https://geopolitique.eu/en/macron-grand-continent/.
8 Ibid.

Chapter 12 Reweaving the social fabric

1 Christopher Caldwell, 'A Bellow from France: why don't Americans "get" Michel Houellebecq, the most important European novelist of the last quarter-century?', *Commentary*, March 2020, https://www.commentary magazine.com/articles/houellebecq-on-the-modern-age/.

2 Here I am indebted to conversations with Jon Cruddas.

3 Jonathan Lear, *Radical Hope: Ethics in the Face of Cultural Devastation* (Cambridge, MA: Harvard University Press, 2008), p. 83.

4 Kantar Public, *Trapped in a Bubble: An Investigation into Triggers for Loneliness in the UK* (London: British Red Cross and Co-op, 2016).

5 Pope Francis, 'A crisis reveals what is in our hearts', *The New York Times*, 26 November 2020, https://www. nytimes.com/2020/11/26/opinion/pope-francis-covid. html.

6 Jonathan Sacks, *Morality: Restoring the Common Good in Divided Times* (London: Basic Books, 2020).

7 Sherry Turkle, *Alone Together: Why We Expect More from Technology and Less from Each Other* (London: Hachette, 2011); *Reclaiming Conversation: The Power of Talk in a Digital Age* (New York: Penguin, 2015).

8 John Gray, in conversation with Kirsty Young on BBC Radio 4's *Desert Island Discs*, 16 March 2018, https:// www.bbc.co.uk/programmes/b09v0xbj.

9 Quoted in Rutherford's excellent essay 'No wealth but life: the conservative origins of English socialism'.

10 Milbank, 'In triplicate: Britain after Brexit; the world after coronavirus; retrospect and prospect'.

11 Danny Kruger MP, 'Levelling up our communities', https://www.dannykruger.org.uk/communities-report.

12 See Pabst, *The Demons of Liberal Democracy*, pp. 100–28.

13 Nancy Fraser, 'From progressive neoliberalism to Trump – and beyond', *American Affairs*, I/4 (Winter 2017): 46–64.

14 Cruddas, *The Dignity of Labour.*
15 The Nuffield Trust, 'What can England learn from the long-term care system in Germany?', 11 September 2019, https://www.nuffieldtrust.org.uk/research/what-can-england-learn-from-the-long-term-care-system-in-germany.
16 Field, 'Rebuilding Beveridge'.
17 Hilary Cottam, *Radical Help: How We Can Remake the Relationships between Us and Revolutionise the Welfare State* (London: Virago, 2018).
18 George Monbiot, 'Could this local experiment be the start of a national transformation?', *The Guardian*, 24 January 2019, https://www.theguardian.com/commentisfree/2019/jan/24/neighbourhood-project-barking-dagenham.

Chapter 13 Restoring the common home of nature

1 Michael Gove MP, 'The privilege of public service', Ditchley Annual Lecture, 1 July 2020, https://www.gov.uk/government/speeches/the-privilege-of-public-service-given-as-the-ditchley-annual-lecture.
2 David Blanchflower and David Bell, 'We must act now to shield young people from the economic scarring of Covid-19', *The Guardian*, 22 May 2020, https://www.theguardian.com/society/2020/may/22/we-must-act-now-to-shield-young-people-from-the-economic-scarring-of-covid-19.
3 https://www.wcl.org.uk/call-for-a-national-nature-service.asp.
4 See the letter 'Growing back better' by Wildlife and Countryside Link to the Chancellor of the Exchequer, https://www.wcl.org.uk/assets/uploads/img/files/Letter_presenting_compendium_2.pdf.
5 Anatol Lieven, *Climate Change and the Nation State: The Realist Case* (London: Penguin, 2020).
6 Chris Smaje, *A Small Farm Future: Making the Case for a Society Built Around Local Economies, Self-Provisioning,*

Agricultural Diversity and a Shared Earth (London: Chelsea Green Publishing, 2020).

7 Henry George, *Progress and Poverty: An Inquiry into the Cause of Industrial Depressions and of Increase of Want with Increase of Wealth: The Remedy* (New York: Appleton, 1879).

8 Colin Tudge, *Six Steps Back to the Land: Why We Need Small Mixed Farms and Millions More Farmers* (Cambridge: Green Books, 2016). Cf. Andrew Simms, *Tescopoly: How One Shop Came Out on Top and Why It Matters* (London: Constable, 2007).

9 Ruth Davis, 'A ten-point plan for nature?', https://ruthswriting.wordpress.com/2020/11/19/a-ten-point-plan-for-nature/. Knepp is a 3,500 acre estate just south of Horsham in West Sussex where since 2001 the land, once intensively farmed, has been the object of a rewilding project that pioneers an approach centred on grazing animals and restoring a natural water course, with phenomenal increases in wildlife and habit creation.

10 Ibid.

11 See James Rebanks, *The Shepherd's Life: A Tale of the Lake District* (London: Penguin, 2016) and *English Pastoral: An Inheritance* (London: Allen Lane, 2020).

Chapter 14 Promoting civic internationalism

1 Christopher Coker, *The Rise of the Civilizational State* (Cambridge: Polity, 2019), pp. x–xi.

2 Samuel P. Huntington, 'The clash of civilizations?', *Foreign Affairs*, 72/3 (Summer 1993), pp. 22–49, expanded as *The Clash of Civilizations and the Remaking of World Order* (New York: Simon & Schuster 1996).

3 Quoted in Michael Crowley, 'As Biden plans global democracy summit, skeptics say: heal thyself first', *The New York Times*, 31 January 2021, https://www.nytimes.com/2021/01/31/us/politics/biden-democracy-summit.html?referringSource=articleShare.

4 Adrian Pabst, *Liberal World Order and Its Critics:*

210

Civilizational States and Cultural Commonwealths (London: Routledge, 2018) and *The Demons of Liberal Democracy.*

5 John Darwin, *After Tamerlane: The Rise and Fall of Global Empires, 1400–2000* (London: Penguin, 2007), p. 19; Bruno Maçães, *The Dawn of Eurasia: On the Trail of the New World Order* (London: Penguin, 2019).

6 Amitav Acharya, *The End of American World Order* (Cambridge: Polity, 2014); Oliver Stuenkel, *Post-Western World: How Emerging Powers are Remaking Global Order* (Cambridge: Polity, 2016).

7 Adrian Pabst, 'China, Russia and the return of the civilizational state', *New Statesman*, 8 May 2019, pp. 24–7, https://www.newstatesman.com/2019/05/china-russia-and-return-civilisational-state; Aris Roussinos, 'The irresistible rise of the civilisation-state: Western liberalism has no answer to assertive powers that take pride in their cultural roots', *UnHerd*, 6 August 2020, https://unherd.com/2020/08/the-irresistible-rise-of-the-civilisation-state/.

8 Groupe d'études géopolitiques, 'The Macron Doctrine'.

9 Coker, *The Rise of the Civilizational State*, p. 90.

10 Groupe d'études géopolitiques, 'The Macron Doctrine'.

11 Quoted from 'Treaty of Adrianople – charges against Viscount Palmerston', Hansard, Vol 97, debated on Wednesday, 1 March 1848, https://hansard.parliament.uk/Commons/1848-03-01/debates/2221a5d7-21f5-49c5-a64a-cc333b61d517/TreatyOf Adrianople—ChargesAgainstViscountPalmerston.

12 Robert Colls, 'What sport teaches us about who we are and where we belong', *New Statesman*, 4 November 2020, https://www.newstatesman.com/politics/sport/2020/11/what-sport-teaches-us-about-who-we-are-and-where-we-belong.

13 See once more Glasman, 'As globalisation fractures, the West must champion internationalism in the face of China'.

14 Ibid.

15 Ross Douthat, *The Decadent Society: How We Became the Victims of Our Own Success* (New York: Simon & Schuster, 2020).
16 Groupe d'études géopolitiques, 'The Macron Doctrine'.
17 See my *Liberal World Order and Its Critics*, pp. 63–80.
18 Christopher Coker, *The Improbable War: China, the United States and the Logic of Great Power Conflict* (London: Hurst, 2014); Graham Allison, *Destined for War: Can America and China Escape Thucydides's Trap?* (Boston, MA: Houghton Mifflin Harcourt, 2017).

Epilogue: a new battleground of ideas

1 Gramsci, 'The Third Notebook (1930)', pp. 32–3.
2 Arnie Graf, *Lessons Learned: Stories from a Lifetime of Organizing* (Chicago: ACTA Publications, 2020).
3 Here I am indebted to conversations with Maurice Glasman and Richard Beardsworth.
4 Amanda Tattersall, *Power in Coalition: Strategies for Strong Unions and Social Change* (Ithaca, NY: Cornell University Press, 2010); Marc Stears, *Out of the Ordinary: How Everyday Life Inspired a Nation and How It Can Again* (Cambridge, MA: Harvard University Press, 2021).

Index

Index

Index

Index

cooperation
  based on shared interests 87, 111
  confederal 100, 174
  international 4, 20, 30, 35, 120, 138–9, 175–6, 178–9, 186, 188
  and trust 5, 18, 31, 78, 97, 103, 129, 180, 189–90
corporatism 117
  communitarianism and postliberalism 4, 21, 31
  corporatist bargaining following Covid-19 100, 135, 137–9, 141
  democratic 4, 99, 134, 135, 137–9, 143, 174, 187
  EU 139–43
  state/non-statist 99
corruption 44, 89, 181
cosmopolitanism 33, 85, 181
covenant ix, 148, 181, 190, 191
  civic ix, 178
  reciprocal 19, 72
  social viii, 152, 168
Covid-19 viii, 9, 27
  Brexit and Covid-19 125, 176
  China 11
  and community 1, 6, 25, 73, 147, 150, 186, 188
  and corporatism 135, 138
  crisis 23–4, 29, 62, 129, 135, 146, 149, 159, 165
  dominant response to 16, 33, 121, 123
  emergency 67
  limits of ideologies ix
  pandemic 1, 3, 6, 12, 23, 25, 26, 27, 55, 68, 170
  post-Covid-19 recovery and reconstruction 128, 140, 143, 159, 162
  post-Covid-19 world 106, 128
  vaccine 176, 178

Cowley, Jason 17, 194
creativity 87, 108
Crick, Bernard 64–5, 189
Cruddas, Jon 157
'culture wars' viii, 50, 63
Cummings, Dominic 60

Davies, William 60–1
Davis, Ruth 165–6
decency 1, 24, 26–7
demagogy 2, 35, 62, 187
democracy viii, 40, 45, 71, 78, 85, 93, 104–5, 114, 130, 134, 163, 170, 177–8
  associative 97
  authoritarian, managed 38
  Chinese movement 15
  Christian 21–2
  and citizenship 38, 85, 87–93, 105
  decentralized/devolved 89, 100, 135, 152, 158, 191
  deliberative 152
  economic 137
  Lasch's *Revolt of the Elites and the Betrayal of Democracy* 80
  liberal 14, 19, 88, 171
  pluralist 31, 62, 100, 106, 117
  renewal of 2, 87, 190
  social 136
  Western 2
  workplace 96, 139, 187
Deneen, Patrick 17
deregulation 21
devolution viii, 92, 135, 174
dictatorship 34, 93
dignity 6, 18, 19, 21, 27, 53, 63, 87, 153
  of labour/work 7, 15, 28, 85, 104, 128, 173, 186, 191
  of the person 43, 51, 76, 96, 103, 104, 118, 143, 172, 177, 182
  in the workplace 129

216

Index

dispossession 27, 49, 118
Dostoevsky, Fyodor 34, 44
Douthat, Ross 13
duties 84, 88
  beget rights 4, 19, 88
  and citizenship 89
  civic 83
  economic 137
  international 83
  mutual/reciprocal 32, 135
  and status 85
Dworkin, Ronald 58, 88, 95

ecology 30, 51, 53, 110–11,
  113–14, 159, 165, 166
  ecological balance ix, 5, 22,
  28, 86, 108
  ecological crisis 62, 160,
  162, 164, 177
  ecological politics 114
  ecological purpose 28–9
  ecological resilience 162
  civic/institutional 100, 125,
  133
The Economist 7
Edgerton, David 125
education 39, 62, 96, 106,
  118, 125, 127, 152, 191
  into citizenship 89, 114, 167
  civic groups 100
  Higher Education/Further
  Education 138
  policies 21
  as a (relational) good 103,
  111
  through-life 129, 187
egalitarianism 36
  see also equality
elites 51, 84, 85
  Brahmin Left and Merchant
  Right 39
  corrupt 8
  and insurgents 2
  Lasch's *Revolt of the Elites*
  80–1, 89

leading by example/virtuous
  137, 190
liberal 14
new/insurgent 2, 130
old 31, 39, 83
plutocratic 41
technocratic 44
employment 88, 118, 128, 129,
  137, 155, 161
'end of history' 121
Enlightenment 33, 72, 76, 182
entitlement(s) 58, 60, 88, 191
equality 36, 38, 51, 63, 76, 87
  abstract 70
  in relation to liberty and
  fraternity 17, 20, 52, 76,
  88, 93
  of restraint 82
  as sameness 19, 69
ethos 138, 142, 187, 190
European Union (EU) 139–43,
  176–8
everyday economy 21, 24, 117,
  126, 129, 131, 133
executive 91, 92, 97, 100, 135,
  174

Facebook 37, 43, 130
fairness 69, 71, 74
  Rawlsian ground-rules of
  88, 95
family viii, 1, 6, 16, 36, 46, 51,
  63, 73, 78, 80, 81, 87–9,
  94, 102, 147, 148, 186–9
  and community and work
  127, 149, 151, 191
  Genovesi on 99
  policy 21, 152–4
  values of 153
  wage 128, 133, 187
far-left/far-right 8, 52, 149, 182
fascism 99, 145, 152, 157,
  188, 191
federalism 139
feminism 70

217

Index

Index

Index

Index

and corporatism 143, 174
democratic viii, 134–5
liberal 17, 28, 34, 37, 104
value 61, 70, 75–6,
Poland 14, 21, 177
Polanyi, Karl 110, 120
populism 12, 14, 20, 45, 66,
  92, 140, 191
anti-elite 91
and authoritarianism viii, 3,
  15, 51, 63, 170, 185
liberal 2, 92, 105–6
and liberalism 15, 145
postliberalism vii, ix, 17,
  19–20, 29, 51, 90, 114,
  188, 190
antiliberal 50
communitarian 3–5
and community 21, 86
corporatist 21,
distorted 50
economic 110
and political pluralism 93
public philosophy of 52, 53,
  79, 89, 108, 110
poverty 1, 128
professional-managerial class 5,
  26, 39, 41, 84
profit 31, 110, 127, 142, 156,
  164
progress 39, 62, 69, 81, 150
Enlightenment 33
faith in 42, 69
propaganda
protectionism 14, 29, 121–2,
  136, 173, 179
Putin, Vladimir 171, 177

rationality/reason 33, 61, 70,
  71, 74
Rawls, John 58, 71, 77, 88,
  95, 120
Raz, Joseph 95
reciprocity 51, 59, 87, 89, 120,
  135, 136, 164, 190

recognition see mutual
  recognition
're-education' camps, China
  93–4
relationships 6, 12, 20, 63,
  66, 73, 76–7, 87, 89, 113,
  129, 145, 148–9, 188–90
and institutions 3, 55, 68,
  71–2, 74, 78, 79, 98,
  100–1, 105, 127, 144,
  147, 174
responsibilities 92, 135, 153,
  187
rights ix, 29, 38, 43, 58, 70,
  76, 129, 172
duties 4, 88, 89
individual 4, 17, 19, 20, 27,
  36, 72, 88, 95, 96, 135
liberalism 76, 111
of minorities 3, 147
and obligations 97, 114,
  118, 135, 148, 190
Roosevelt, Franklin D. 159–60
Rousseau, Jean-Jacques 50, 77
Roussinos, Aris 41
royal colleges 129, 133
Rubio, Marco 48
rule of law 17, 20, 36, 61, 71,
  83, 78, 181
Russia 14, 35, 38, 40, 41, 169,
  171, 172, 176–8, 182–3
Rutherford, Jonathan 71

sacredness 69, 173
Sandel, Michael 20
Scruton, Roger 49, 114
self-government 15, 56, 130,
  141
self-interest 6, 37, 83, 88, 96,
  150, 180, 189, 190
social cohesion 4, 18, 62, 70
social contract 19, 72, 77, 95
social Darwinism 62
social democracy 136
social engineering 34, 58, 81

221

Index

Index

Index